# IMMORTA

BEING SPIRIT BOOK THREE

# IMMORTAL SPIRIT

## YOU ARE SPIRIT IN HUMAN FORM

CHANNELLED BY JANET NEVILLE
WRITTEN BY STEVE BRIDGER

T

Troubador Publishing Ltd
Unit E2 Airfield Business Park
Harrison Road, Market Harborough
Leicestershire LE16 7UL
Tel: 0116 279 2299
Email: books@troubador.co.uk
Web: www.troubador.co.uk

ISBN 978 1 83628 046 0

British Library Cataloguing in Publication Data.
A catalogue record for this book is available from the British Library.

Printed and bound in Great Britain by 4edge Limited
Typeset in 12pt Garamond by Troubador Publishing Ltd, Leicester, UK

We would like to dedicate this book to our Spirit Guides and
ALLAN WATT
&
EDNA LUCY BRIDGER

Heartfelt thanks to:
Rosie Halliday
Suzi Cartwright
Isabelle Dubois
Cindy Théodor
Michael Djan
Gilly Hall
Bernadete May
Denise & Les Pilgrim
Eugene Slattery

spirit@beingspirits.com
https://www.beingspirits.com

# Contents

Appendices

# Earth Side and Spirit Side

*Immortal Spirit* has two interlinked sections. The first will focus on your life in the here and now. It will take you through the cycle of spiritual life along with the psychic tools to communicate with Spirit.

Spirit Side enters another world. It will widen your perception of the twin life you lead. Life on earth is but a station on your way.

We are human and spiritual beings at one and the same time.

# Reader Reactions

Immortal Spirit *Review – Gordon Robertson, 31 March 2024*

Hi, Steve! As ever, the book is a revelation, a real eye-opener. Even having had the experience of reading the first two books, there was still so much of the Spirit world that was unknown to me. And no doubt still is!

The most extraordinary thing about this book is the depth it goes into regarding life on 'the other side'. Spirit really does take pains to explain it in terms that earthbound humans will understand. And it does so with a strong, reassuring sense of compassion, compassion that runs throughout the whole book, real compassion from benevolent beings towards us less-than-perfect mortals. That in itself is a valuable lesson to take away. We are all one, so why do we treat others as less than ourselves? It doesn't make sense, and yet it happens all too often. Perhaps the messages delivered via this book will change all that.

The Soul Rescue section is a fascinating glimpse into an area of spirituality I doubt many are aware of and furthers the bond between both sides of the spiritual divide. It also reiterates the necessity of belief, not in one particular religion, but in the eternal oneness we are all a part of. The personal stories in this section bring a welcome sense of familiarity to the book as well. We all know people who have passed in tragic ways; we just didn't know what happened to them after that. This section is a gateway to our understanding in that regard. In fact, the book as a whole is a gateway to our understanding of the fundamentals of spirituality.

And for that alone, it should be applauded.

Ten out of ten, sir! Please pass on my congratulations to Janet and the other Mediums. I wish you all only the best for the book's success. Love and best wishes, Gordon.

### *Maria Hennings Reaction, 4 June 2024*

Hiya, Steve, first of all, thank you for letting me read the book prior to publication and I am so sorry it's taken me so long to read and get back to you with a review – my daughter got married last Monday – and it's been such a mad couple of months getting everything organised and I just didn't have as much time to dedicate to the book as I would have liked and I was aware that you're probably waiting for the reviews to come in, so I have read it – albeit rather quickly and in binge sessions, so I hope this is helpful!

Anyway – here's my thoughts: I have always been interested in 'the other side' and the concept of Mind Body Spirit – ever since I read *Living Magically* by Gillian Edwards many, many years ago. I particularly enjoyed the way you bring Spirit into everyday understanding and the details you give about what it takes to be a Medium. I think for many the Spirit world can be intimidating and scary – but your book tells us that we have no need to be afraid of anything as we are being looked after at all times, even though sometimes it doesn't 'feel' like it! I would really like to read the book again (more slowly, so that

I can savour it), but as a hard copy so that I can underline and highlight passages that I think are really significant and make the book my own reference guide to the Spirit world. xxx

# Introduction

We welcome you.

Spirit wanted us to pass on their love and learning by opening this window to your thoughts. This book is about your personal, innermost spirituality. It is about the very essence of you.

No matter where you live, whichever God you worship, which religion or faith you follow, the colour of your skin or cultural roots, gay, straight or unsure. This book is for everyone. We are all Spirit.

These are the words of one of our guides, Sister Theresa:

*We are all worshipping the same God. We all need to tune into our own spirituality. If this means that you are following another religion, it doesn't matter because you are working on your own spirituality.*

We'd like to introduce one of our Spirit Guides to say an opening prayer. It's from Guiding Light. These are his words channelled through Janet.

*Imagine your mind is an empty vessel, all the words that were there have tumbled out. Imagine that empty vessel is filling up with light and that you're being consumed with the power of Spirit. The Spirit that is within and around you. The same Spirit that we are. From our world to your world, my friend, we open up this book so we can bring love and affection, hope, courage, and wisdom so you can move on in your life.*

*The purpose of these books is to pass on the knowledge we have in our world. We give this knowledge to you in order for you to learn and understand.*

*Enjoy the touch of the spiritual energy that is being delivered to you from our world.*

*Amen.*

We are all psychic. Every human has the ability to communicate with Spirit. It is achieved by opening a channel of mind and thought. This connects with Spirit's invisible presence to experience their love and support.

You may already follow a positive and loving code of living with a conventional religion or belief of faith. What you are about to read flows directly from the spiritual realms. It is not intended to challenge or conflict with any belief you may already hold. Spirit wanted us to use these pages to provide knowledge. Not to preach or convert.

The book content has been received from Spirit by Janet Neville, who is a Spiritual Medium. She is the communication channel between two worlds. Our world and the invisible spiritual realms surround us. Messages from Spirit have been added exactly as received without editorial changes. You could refer to these messages as 'Letters from Heaven' as they are from divine energies such as guides, angels and highly evolved celestial beings.

These words were channelled by Medium Les Pilgrim from his guide, Brother John. They beautifully capture how spirituality is the essence of our existence: One Love, One Truth, One Light.

*The concept that we all have to have a religion to believe in God is an unnecessary burden to carry. Above all else, One Love, One Truth, and One Light overrides all systems of faith and worship.*

*Granted that everyone has the freedom of choice to follow a particular belief, but that does not mean you are any better than a non-believer or supporter of any other philosophy.*

*In your world, there's discord and strife among individuals and nations. If one believes in the absolute truth that love conquers all and that God loves us all, then we can become the complete, harmonious, spiritual beings on earth that the divine Spirit would want us to be.*

*It does not matter one iota what is your faith, your chosen rituals or form of worship. It is plain and simple to share the beautiful gifts we all receive from Spirit and utilise them for the sake of humanity and be worthy of the love of the Divine.*

*Brother John*

Our aim is for you to:

- Realise your true nature as Spirit in human form.
- Open your mind to the immortal cycle of everlasting life.
- Provide assurance that family and friends you've lost still exist in Spirit, loving and caring for you.
- Accept your vital role as a custodian and protector of this beautiful planet.

*Australian Aboriginal Proverb*

We are all visitors to this time, this place.
We are just passing through.
Our purpose here is to observe, to learn, to grow, to love
And then
We return home.

*Introducing the authors*

Janet and Steve

We thought we would explain how Spirit, Janet, and I work together.

Spirit is the powerhouse of energy in the creative process. Their influence is a real, tangible, guiding force. Spirits are our coaches and our direct source of information. Janet is the first point of contact in receiving the book content. This is achieved when she enters a higher state of consciousness to connect with her guides and other spiritual energies. They speak through her vocal cords for me to record and pass onto you.

These energies have become firm friends. They give us their names, and we recognise their personalities. Over the years, this has helped us identify their widely different characteristics. Energies can be recognised by what they say and how they say it. They feel for us. They know when we are feeling down or stressed. They encourage us as spiritual partners.

They tell us their stories. Guides have lived on earth. They describe their time here, about where and when they lived, their families and how they passed into Spirit. These are true life stories. They speak to us as friends and colleagues. They are invisible, but their presence is clearly felt.

My role as writer is to shape the chapter structure and create the narrative flow. Spirit drop the seed of thought into my mind to trigger my fingers on the computer keyboard.

Running Water, Janet's principal guide, said these words before we started writing *Immortal Spirit*.

*Running Water, 23 January 2023*

> *We know you want to start your new book. We know it has been going around in your mind for quite a while. You feel you are coming to a halt. We do not want things to be a big chore for you. It will happen, it will happen when you are ready to be able to do this. We said that you would be inundated with much material. And that it would be to your benefit to file it away in order for when you need it. We know there are far too many pages for you to continually read through.*
>
> *At times the way things are planned within your mind have alterations and go along a different route. It is quite exciting, Stephen, when things take a turn from where you expected it. This is going to happen. We just want you to enjoy what is to come. We want you to enjoy what you are doing. At this moment in time, you have helped many people. You have helped Michael. At the same time, Michael is helping you, giving you more information from his guides and the energies that come through who have taken their time for their energies to blend with him and be able to go through his thoughts and his mind.*

*It is like going through a jigsaw puzzle to un-jumble the pieces or work out a knitting pattern to make it make sense. The guides are working busily away. Every meeting you have you are learning all the time. That goes for all of you. Every time you sit, the energies are there. One small piece or morsel of information comes through. We know we are repetitive but we need to be in order for it to penetrate into people's minds and for them to remember the teaching.*

*All the information we pass on is for you to remember and share with other people. This is our job, and it is your job, too, when you started to work alongside us.*

*You do not have to force it into people's minds. It is when people approach you with interest, you can answer any questions because of all the information stored within your own mind. Your mind is better than any computer mankind can ever make. It is being stored in your own memory back in the very deep and dark recesses of your mind. When you come back to Spirit, it is there. It is like a big filing cabinet.*

*Everything you learnt in your lifetime is there within a small, tiny chip in your memory. It is there. It starts to come alive when you come back to Spirit. You will think,* 'Where does all this come from? How do people develop and progress from everything they've discovered and everything that was new to them at the time?' *It's all stored in your mind so when you come back, it's all there for you to revisit and embellish. That's where the advancements and great achievements come from. That's where you can pass it down to earth into someone's thoughts.*

*Life is a cycle. Life is eternity. So is knowledge. Knowledge is eternal. People never mention that. They just say that life is continuous. Life is everlasting. Once your lifetime on earth has finished, it continues in the spiritual realms. Knowledge is eternal, my friend, as knowledge has been passed around and around. Knowledge goes within that circle as well. It is being passed around and embellished upon. Knowledge grows and grows until it gets to the point where the advancement on your earth happens. It starts from within your minds, within the earth, until it comes back to the spiritual realms, where it gets passed back round. That is the everlasting cycle of knowledge. It is passed from one thought to another.*

Spirit mentioned Michael's name. He is one of several exceptional Mediums that Janet has helped develop their higher consciousness, including Suzi, Rosie, Gilly and Cindy.

# Blog Introduction

Running parallel with the chapters are blog passages taken from our website, beingspirits.com. The idea is to provide extra comment and insight into different aspects of spirituality. Read them when the desire takes you. The blogs may repeat points raised in the chapter content. Repetition is not a bad thing. They have been placed in random order throughout the manuscript. Here's the first:

*Draw Back the Curtain of Doubt*

Understandably, people have misgivings about those who claim they can tell your fortune. Some have the psychic skills to 'read' your mind. They can sense your mood: happy, anxious, worried or stressed. They have the ability to draw a great deal of information about you in your current physical and mental state. These will relate to your worldly, everyday situation.

Spiritual Mediums work differently. They provide proof as they connect with someone who has passed using the gift of clairvoyance. It is the communication channel that links our world with the next. Love is energy. Love remains forever strong. You will be able to identify a person by a detailed description of their physical appearance, their personality and relationship with you. Once you are satisfied with an accurate description, the Medium will pass on a message. The message is for you and you alone.

It probably won't be about a new job or car or even meeting a new love in your life. For certain, it will be to prove your loved one, or ones, care and love you and most importantly of all, that they still exist in mind, thought, and Spirit.

Clairvoyance could be the beginning of your spiritual awakening. Here's a message from Spirit as printed in our second book, *Believe in Spirit.*

> *Communication from our world to yours is to prove that life is eternal. Human Spirit is energy, it is mind and thought. Spirit is indestructible. Spirit lives on continuously. When you are on the earth in a physical body, it is easy to forget that you are Spirit in human form. You are an everlasting spiritual being. The purpose for us is to produce these written words in the hope that whoever reads this can gain a small amount of understanding about the Realms of Spirit.*

### *Sceptic or Cynic?*

If you've reached this sentence, you may be open to accepting ideas that are dismissed by many. A cynic would have rubbished the concept instantly. A sceptic would have doubted it but would be prepared to listen and learn more before passing judgement.

Spirit wants you to ask questions and reach your own conclusions.

## Coming Next

*The Complete You*

This next chapter is for you. It will explore the mortal and immortal elements of your being. You're an incredible combination of energy both inside and outside your physical body. The two elements work in harmony, seen and unseen.

# PART ONE

## Earth Side Chapters

# One

## The Complete You

Visible Invisible Mortal and Immortal. That's You.

Take a look in the mirror. There you are, smiling back. The mirror sees and confirms you as part of the human race. A mortal being.

What doesn't the mirror see? What's hidden inside the glass?

It can't perceive your intelligence, your creativity, your sense of humour, your emotions, your intuition. These fundamental elements are invisible. They are an essential part of you. They exist. The mirror can't see your spiritual self. You know it exists. Spirit transcends mortality. Eventually your body ceases to function. Your spiritual energy lives on.

Guiding Light would like to speak. These are his words from a meeting on 28 January 2023.

*Emotions are you. They make the person. They make the Spirit. The Spirit is you. It's very cleverly done. People ask what is the soul. Is the soul the Spirit or is it something different? Is the soul my personality? You have the soul and you have the Spirit, they are both as one. There are emotions that make up the Spirit and emotions that make up the soul.*

*It's difficult sometimes for people to grasp that. They think they are being governed by the brain and the heart and all the organs that make your body function. They don't realise that if they take that invisible source, their Spirit, away from you, you will not exist. They think it's the brain and the heart that's keeping them going. They think it's the brain that's giving them the emotions and everything that allows them to function as a normal person. Spirit is still there. When Spirit is detached from the body, Spirit still functions. Spirit does not need the body to keep it alive.*

Spirit wants you to know that no matter what skin colour you have, gender you are, whatever sexual orientation, whether you are suffering from sight loss, or deafness, rich or poor, disabled or enabled, autistic, clear of mind or with mental issues.

We are all essentially the same. We are energies learning from this earthly existence. You have embarked on your own earthly, spiritual assault course.

These are words from Black Feathers, a highly evolved energy and member of the Cheyenne tribe:

*I want to speak about time, as time is so important on your earth.*

*The tick of the clock is going every second. It is often said that Spirit have no conception of time. Time is there within the spiritual world, as it is all around you in the atmosphere. It is all linked up with the timing on the earth plane. We are not in a hurry to go anywhere or do anything. You are only on the earth for a certain time. It doesn't matter to us as time is eternal and it is in the ether for the eternal time and links up with the natural resources. In your mind, you may think that you will be on this earth for your eightieth or ninetieth year that is what the mind is telling you because it thinks that's what a lifetime is.*

*My friend, your lifetime, your time on earth, is over when you come back to Spirit. This may be one or two years or many years. Time is not to be wasted, so you must pack in as much as you can. A person can live to a very old age but you can say to that person: 'What have you achieved in your life during all those years?' That person could sit back and think, and they could look at you and say, 'I wish I'd done this or wish I'd done that. I regret not having done something or doing something and not learning by it.' But then you could say to a person of forty or fifty years, and you could say to them, 'What have you achieved?' And they could say, 'I have achieved much greatness. I did so much and learnt how to live with other people and how their energies can blend together, and I learnt something valuable that is we are all on this earth together, and none of us know when we are going to leave the earth.*

*'I learnt that we should all live together in as much harmony and peace and goodwill, as much as we possibly can. As such, time is irrelevant when related to how long we are on the earth it is what we do with that time while you are there. This is what people tend to forget.'*

Let's return to the 'assault course' theme.

We all know life is full of ups and downs, of pleasure and pressures. Often, they come without warning. It's how we handle them that tests us. That last sentence was easy to write but the reality of life can be beyond traumatic or ecstatic. It is what we learn and how the lessons shape us that are the challenges during the assault course of life for good and not so good. Our energy centres play an essential role during this passage of time.

### *Spiritual Energy Centres – Chakras and Auras*

The title of this chapter is 'The Complete You'. We've said that you are Spirit in human form. To end this chapter, here is an explanation of the energy centres around your body. These complete the spiritual element of your identity as a spiritual being. They are your chakras and your aura.

Together, they complete the internal and external energy centres inside and around our bodies. Each has seven progressively linked positions. These energies are forever active. They spiritually mirror the human body.

Chakra layers actively combine to heighten spiritual consciousness within. Put another way, it's as if energy builds and develops in seven upward steps to your higher self. Each step melding, blending, with the next. They work together simultaneously.

*Table 1: Chakra Positions*

| No | Colour | Position |
|---|---|---|
| 1 | Red | Pelvic area |
| 2 | Orange | Below the navel |
| 3 | Yellow | Solar plexus |
| 4 | Green | At the heart centre |
| 5 | Blue | At the throat |
| 6 | Indigo | Third Eye – in the centre of your forehead |
| 7 | Purple | Top centre of your head – the crown |

What do the chakra positions relate to?

1st Red Root at the base of our spine. Is the focal point of grounding, stability and sense of security. Of being centred.

2nd Orange Sacral is in the lower abdomen. Links with sexuality and creative energy. It relates with your emotions and emotional interactions with others.

3rd Yellow Solar Plexus is just below the rib cage and is associated with your self-confidence, the view of yourself, of your personal esteem.

4th Green Heart Chakra is at the centre of the chest. Love, personal relationships, personal development and life direction.

5th Blue Throat Chakra communications, of speaking your inner truth.

6th Indigo is the Third Eye position in the centre of your forehead between the brow. It is the centre of your intuition, perception and imagination. It is the focal point of your spiritual seeing-eye.

7th Purple is at the crown of your head. It is the point of connection with Spirit and your spirituality.

*Auras*

Auras form seven ethereal layers that surround our physical bodies. Imagine your body being encapsulated in these strands of translucent protective energy. The importance of auras is not always appreciated. If you look at the picture and follow Table 2 you will see that layers one to three have physical links. From four to seven, the higher dimensions of your soul's journey are revealed.

As you transcend from incarnation to reincarnation, your aura remains with you. As you progress and slowly climb the golden ladder to become as one with the Divine, your aura is your spiritual record charting your progress.

*Table 2: Auric Layers Around Your Body*

| Layer | Name | Position | Meaning | Colour |
|---|---|---|---|---|
| 1 | Etheric | Closer to the body | Physicality | Blueish-Grey |
| 2 | Emotional | Second from the body | Emotions & Feelings | Many colours Changes with moods and health |
| 3 | Mental | Third from the body | Thoughts & State of mind | Bright Yellow |
| 4 | Astral | Fourth from the body | Connection to Astral Travelling | Pink or Rose Coloured |
| 5 | Etheric Template | Fifth from the body | Represents the body blueprint on this plane | Colour changes with mood/health |
| 6 | Celestial | Sixth from the body | The link with the Divine | Pearly White |
| 7 | Ketheric Template | Seventh furthest from the body. | Feeling as one with the universe. Holds all the information about your soul and previous lifetimes. | Gold |

Never forget how exceptional you are. This combination of the physical and spiritual makes you unique. In the pages that follow, you'll see what strength, compassion, and potential you possess. Whatever you believe in, believe in yourself and the ability to change the world.

## Blog

*Be Yourself – Everyone Else is Taken*

I stole that headline. It was attributed to Oscar Wilde, the famous Irish writer, poet and playwright. It fits beautifully with the theme of reconnecting to your inner self and revisiting the very core of your being. The idea is to vanquish low self-esteem, self-doubt and any misguided feelings of failure.

As a spiritual being, you have love, care and compassion built into your soul. Living in these years, we are both blessed and cursed with technology. Our interaction with each other is often through radio waves and devices that allow us to hide our intensely personal feelings.

It's easy to become so reliant on technology and swept up in the hustle of daily life. You may have reached a certain point then pressed the 'stop' button. Don't self-limit. You're here to experience so much. Don't stand and watch as life flies past.

Love yourself. Listen to your body. Your soul may be crying out for attention. Here are some exercises for a good workout in the spiritual gym of life:

- Make physical contact (preferably eye-to-eye) with someone, especially someone who is feeling low and needs you.

- Be there to guide a friend through dark times. Reach out if you spot any signs of depression or unhappiness.
- Be true to yourself. Feel alive. Shine your light.

## Coming Next

*The Spiritual Cycle of Life*

The words of the Archangel Michael welcome you to the next chapter. It's true. Celestial beings do make contact as well as guides from ancient times and cultures from around the world. 'The Spiritual Cycle of Life' will provide an insight into what being immortal holds for today and the future.

# Two

# The Spiritual Cycle of Life

Archangel Michael wanted to share these thoughts as he saw our little group working with Spirit:

*We bring prayers to the world, my friend. I flap my wings as people see them with a golden hue. It is something depicted by man thousands of years ago; someone had a vision of a serene figure with translucent wings. Over the years, it has transpired that we do have golden wings. But in actual fact, I am simply a Spirit. I want to wish glad tidings to each and every one of you. I wanted to come and visit your group as it has been some time since my visitation has come and become part of your group. I am here as a comforter and as your protector. Also, I come to converse and help you within your minds of where you are going.*

*Each and every one of you is on a journey and your journeys are all different, very individual to yourselves; even though you are working as one together, your pathways are in different avenues. There is a big golden light above this circle; it is quite dazzling. There are many spirits around; they are all coming to let you know they are there and working with you. I want to speak again about the pathways you have chosen. You would not have chosen them while you were on the earth plane. They were planned in advance when you were in Spirit.*

*We all want to work together so that we can trust the work we are doing and that you can deliver the messages and the love in the way we so much want it to be done and developed. Development is a very important subject to be speaking of. The development of a person is very important. Everyone develops at a different rate and we urge people not to develop too quickly and too soon. If you develop too quickly it gets taken away from you because you are not learning or understanding of what everything is about. If you develop at a slow pace, it is all absorbed within your mind and within your energy.*

This next piece is central to your understanding and acceptance of what it means to be immortal. To know for certain that spiritual life continues after physical death. This can be confirmed by Spiritual Mediums. They provide personal and private evidence that only you know to be true. And of course, they have never met you before or know anything about you.

There is an ultimate magnificent power beyond our comprehension. The creator of the universe. A supreme being. God, if you prefer. It is the magnitude that lies at the heart of all man-made religions and at our very existence. The God particle lives within you. It is sublime, indestructible energy.

What form does immortality take? If you could see it, what would it look like?

The answer is pure energy. It's like an invisible capsule of consciousness. Energy that contains all the markers of your identity, intelligence, character, personality, knowledge and memory. It's your individual spiritual core. The epicentre of your being. Some would say your soul.

*Have we gone off-track?*

Not really. Reincarnation has a purpose. You are immortal for a reason. This particular life cycle was probably not your first visit to this planet.

The ultimate aim is for you to become spiritually whole and as one with the Divine. Every life you lead is an upward point on your learning curve. When it's over, you will return to Spirit and the Spirit world, you will assess what you've learnt and prepare to do it again at some point in the future. Needless to say, this whole process takes time. There's more to come in Chapter Eight – 'The Realms of Spirit'.

Mary has these points to make about your essential immortality:

*It is often said upon your earth what happens when you die. People say 'nothing'. Your body goes into the earth or into the furnace and that's the end of that. Because they feel your brain is the functioning part of your mind. So, when the brain dies, they feel that everything dies along with it. How wrong they are, my friend.*

*It's a revelation when they come back to Spirit to realise and find out that their brain, after all, what was part of your physical body contains the Spirit that was living within that part of the anatomy and it was also the spiritual essence as well.*

*Obviously, the brain does have something to do with the way everything was functioning, their eyes, their speaking, their movement but it is that tiny speck of energy that no one can see that is your Spirit, your soul. It is there deep within you.*

*It's like that tiny dot that makes up you the person, the whole of you. It is the thoughts in your mind that urge you on. The footsteps from night to day to the tomorrow that keep you moving forward and forward.*

*Everyone functions at different rates. People think differently. You have the words, the vocabulary in your mind but you use them completely differently from one person to the next. We all have the same basic wants and needs but you all juggle about with them from one person to the next. When a person comes back, when that essence of that tiny Spirit comes back into our world, it is like another awakening for them, another re-birth. It is that rebirth of having to go through the life that they have just led on the earth. All of a sudden, the revelation comes to them of how they used that life on the earth. It will happen to you.*

*At times when you are walking on the earth as you are now, that you are mixing with different people, there is so much negativity energy going all around you. You have what people call the lay-lines that make disturbances. They can lift you up and bring you down. And you also have love. Love is the positive energy that everyone needs. Love always conquers hate. Light always conquers dark. With people, the energy comes back to our world, it is not only a revelation that their mind is still in existence.*

*It is a revelation of how I wished I did something different with my life. How I wish I had gone down that pathway instead of this pathway. How I wish I used my words completely differently when I spoke to a certain person. How I regret how my words affected that person without me realising. I could go on and on, my friend. It is about beliefs. Not everybody believes in our world or about other religions. It is important for someone to have a belief in something. If a person says they are an atheist, do they believe in anything? They have to believe in themselves when using those words. Yes, they do believe in something. They just don't know what they believe at that moment in time.*

*Our world is full of peace. It's a working world as well because we continue to strive forward all the time. We work with the light. There are dark forces. But we are continuously working to push back those forces. We are always learning. No matter how old an energy is, we are always learning. We can teach what we have learnt. On the earth you teach your children as it is important to be able to teach someone. How do we know if we are teaching them in the correct manner? It is no different when you are back in the spiritual realms.*

*Our energies have learnt an awful lot from living on your planet but we keep striving forward. When we work with you, we are blending our energies with you. We come as close as we possibly can. We give you our knowledge to pass down. We do not push you. We do not tell you what to do. It is important that you have your own choices. This is how you learn. You learn from your mistakes. It is important to learn from your mistakes. It is important to show sorrow if you have hurt someone through your words or actions. Or if you have caused unnecessary grief or upset.*

With those thoughts from Mary in mind. Perhaps you could:

- Reconnect with the child inside and savour the little things that have been blotted out by growing up.
- Feel the warmth of being with close friends or the triumph of a simple action or accomplishment that makes you glow with pride.
- Perform a random act of kindness to someone. Keep it secret to yourself, a private pleasure. See the thanks in their eyes for your unexpected action.
- Dare to change, to try something new. It may have been daunting and off-putting until now. You have the determination inside to help you succeed.
- Treat yourself. Relish those favourite places and sounds, sunsets, music, singing. Lose yourself in art, dance round the kitchen, anything and everything that enriches your senses. Anything that gives you joy.

That last point, 'Treat Yourself', is extremely important. During this lifetime, feel your senses acutely. Your mortal body is experiencing all these wonderful sensations. They're logged into your memory. When you return to Spirit, they'll form part of your store of recollections. They're part of your increasing bank of knowledge that will shape your spiritual progress.

Incarnation another view:

Spirit like to repeat themselves to make sure we understand their lessons like good teachers do. They've asked us to return to the theme of incarnation. We first introduced incarnation in *Being Spirit* with our guide, The Scribe, using the Sunflower and its seeds to represent the several lifetimes one person could experience. One seed for one lifetime to complete a full face of the flower.

Another way of expressing the concept was used by Shakespeare. He adopted a very human approach.

As You Like It – *Act 2 Scene 7*

> *All the world's a stage, and all the men and women merely players. They have their exits and their entrances; and one man in his time plays many parts.*

Human spirits are eternal. The spiritual cycle evolves over many unique lifetimes. You would take on a different role in the never-ending play of spiritual life. Every lifetime would be a fresh new story. New script, new plot, new characters, new mental and emotional challenges in the evolution of your Spirit. Your soul would retain fragments of memory of previous existences.

This performance is your lifetime. Every day shapes our being. We're acting a part from the drama of our birth to the final curtain. We exit stage left and rejoin the world of Spirit to begin rehearsals for our next incarnation. The time spent in the realms would be a continuous learning and development process before we take on a new, different character in another time on earth.

This may be a change of gender, country, religion, physical and mental attitude, with the influences of good or evil. During the process, it is your decision to remain in the realms or venture anew onto this planet. All the while broadening and fulfilling your spiritual identity.

What would your friends and loved ones think when you've left the stage? Would they remember how you touched their emotions? How you faced your demons? How you grappled and coped with challenges? Would they treasure the gift of love you gave?

These are the words of Spirit:

*The important message here, my friend, is that life is eternal, whatever path you choose. Life on the earth is an experience which many choose to repeat time and time again until they felt they have exhausted every aspect of the human emotions.*

*Each return will be pure and clear, with memories or disturbances from previous lives being erased. It is like a blank canvas waiting for the artist to shape a new story. Every life that returns is precious and to be cherished, to give and receive love and respect your fellow man. My friend, we can only hope and try that one day that will be achieved.*

A parting thought. This is about the life you're living now and will go on to develop in Spirit. Earthly death is at the end of Act Three, and the transition to a new character, a fresh role for the same actor. Your spiritual self is an eternal and complete energy. Be proud of your performance in this production.

## Blog

*Meditation*

### *Tuning Into Spirit*

You're in the zone. You're preparing to meditate. You're feeling prickles of stress induced static leaving your body. Negative energies are slip-sliding away. Your breathing is getting deeper and slower. Your inner self is smiling a welcome to the energy of your mind. Surely this is a sublime spiritual experience? Well, yes and no.

Yes, because the soothing waves are dissipating the curled

nuggets of stress in your head and releasing the coiled tendons of physical muscle. And perhaps you are feeling good inside and feeling the restorative tendrils of healing.

No, because the accent is on the physical benefits. Your energy has been directed inwardly and not outwardly towards Spirit. Please don't misunderstand me. Meditation is an effective tool and a brilliant aid for relaxing prior to making a spiritual connection.

The issue is to recognise the crossover point where you've effectively tuned in to your secret self and switched on to Spirit.

You've been on a wonderful journey into your own mind. It's not enough to think, *I'm now so chilled and relaxed, so spiritual, that I'm ready to connect with Spirit.* Then wonder why nothing happens. Has your guide left you? Have they withdrawn their energies? This will never happen. Put it like this. When you invite Spirit to join you, it's like switching on a light above your head. Spirit sees your light and know it is their signal to join you. It is a special relationship between teacher and student. The invitation from mind to mind has to come from you. Talk to your guide in your head. Talk to them as a friend. They will never judge. There's no formality about speaking with Spirit.

The more you show dedication and commitment by regularly thinking and inviting Spirit to play an active part in your life, the faster you'll develop, the quicker you'll move forward. If your only connection is when you attend a circle meeting, or if your attendance is a bit erratic, don't be surprised if you get the feeling of distance between you and your guides. After all, the connection is a two-way process. You are two spirits working together. Two friends together. Invite them into your life.

That blog was written with the channelled input of Grey Dove Native American Indian.

## Coming Next

*The Language of Thought*

Inquisitiveness is the first step to gaining knowledge. Questioning follows. Do you doubt whether something is true or false? You want evidence, you need proof. Then you decide.

This next chapter will explain how millions of people connect with Spirit every day. These pages will show you how you can explore and embrace your own spirituality. We'll explain the process of linking with Spirit as if you're training to become a Spiritual Medium.

# Three

## The Language of Thought

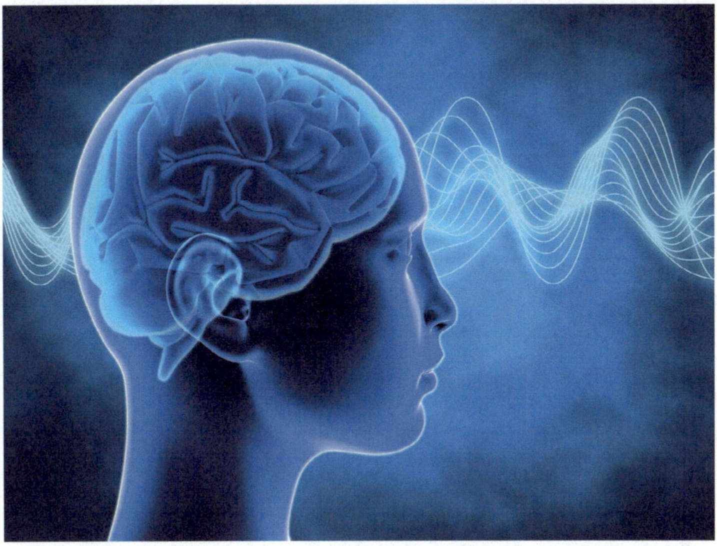

Think of your brain as a transmitter. A conveyor of thought. Linking with Spirit is your mind sending out thought waves to be in tune with their energy. It's like scanning radio waves to reach a crisp spot, a clear signal of connection with the other side of life.

In a nutshell, that's what Mediums do. Easy? Well, no. We are all psychic but it takes time, dedication, lots of practice, maybe over years, to reach that sweet spot. Some find it easier than others. Some expect too much, too soon. It's not like picking up a phone and calling home. You have to be realistic. You have to have trust and respect. And understand that setting up a channel of communication takes love, commitment, patience and time.

I was just about to start explaining about Mediumship in greater detail when I broke away from writing to meet Janet for our regular Friday morning meeting. That's when she connects directly with our Spirit Guides and lets the conversation flow. We never know in advance what the topic of conversation will be. It is something Spirit feels they want to say. They surprise us all the time. This note is from Black Crow:

*We are there with you. The energies are picking up when we are there together. There is much I wish to speak about. We want to keep the meeting short.*

*I would like to talk to you about anger management. That has taken you by surprise, my friend. There are many people here on earth that have that anger management built inside them. It is like a bubble within their soul, their solar plexus. A small piece of anger starts to build and needs to be released. They direct it to other people, sometimes people do not deserve to have that anger being pointed to them. This is what I wanted to speak about.*

*We want to take away that distress. We can call it distress. You have to find your own mantra, my friend, that you can follow. You take yourself off to a room or open space where nature is at its best. You can close your eyes and become one with your Spirit, with your own higher self. That Spirit, that piece of God, is part of the Creator. It is that tiny piece of spiritual guidance that's within you since birth until you come back to the Creator.*

*Try to get a mantra in your head. It is your own mantra. This works with some people and this is what I would like to use if I came back to the earth. I would choose an open space with the sky above me and the twitter of birds. I would close my eyes and loosen everything around me, and let my muscles relax.*

*I would imagine that I'm sitting in a temple where everything is protected and secure. You can create your own colours. I would sit and close my eyes and imagine that everything around me is calm. We have allowed ourselves to be open to the negative energy and be surrounded by the hustle and bustle of life to come upon us. Between myself and my higher self, I would like to draw upon the bright light that is forever around us. I would like to light that flicker of fire that is within me so that light is flickering away. As I'm speaking, it's like me taking myself out of my body and looking back at it. All the colours of the chakras and the colour mauve and indigo would be protecting myself.*

*Gradually, that same positivity and peace would be coming within you and any distress you have within you would flow out of yourself and would be surrounding yourself. The peace would be absorbed within your higher self. For myself, as I got more experienced in this, I would start to recite certain things in my mind. For example, 'I thank you, dear Lord, for the peace and comfort around me. Thank you, dear Lord, for being there and for being my guiding hand to be called upon whenever I wished. I hand over all my anxieties on a plate so that I can become renewed and refreshed.'*

Black Crow's words link perfectly with these next thoughts.

### *Tuning in to Meditation*

In the broadest sense, we can pass on the love of Spirit in our daily lives by caring, showing kindness and giving a helping hand. This is the way of the Spiritual Medium. Developing these skills is a matter of intention. As we've said, we're all psychic. It's how we direct that ability is the thing. It is not to make money as a priority, tell fortunes or boost your ego. It is to work *with* Spirit, as we are Spirit. You are Spirit.

How do we begin? Why not listen to some further advice from Grey Dove, channelled by Janet. In our meetings, it can be months or even years between an energy joining the conversation. Then, like Grey Dove, he's with us and sharing his wisdom in a concentrated way. We need to make the most of him while he's with us:

*Banish material thoughts from your mind as you are about to leave the physical world and join the spiritual world. When people connect with our energies, we like them to be as calm as we can possibly make them. We are about to bathe you in the warm light of Spirit. It's like a tranquil existence that is very hard to understand or imagine until you can actually experience it. All you can hear is her voice with our words.*

*Try to let every muscle in your body relax. Make sure your feet are firmly upon the ground, people would say that you are grounded and as one with the earth. It is the earth from which the energy comes from. Imagine the energy is coming up through the earth and into your core, filling your whole body with the spiritual energy. Relax so you can feel calm and be ready to intertwine your energies with our energies.*

*From the Creator, from the Divine, we not only bathe you in the light of Spirit, but we bathe you within the protection and the love of the Lord. We can allow this meeting to commence so we can fill your head, your mind, with words of wisdom, words of courage, words of knowledge from the energies here that are all around you, that surround you. Imagine that you've been elevated from one room to another. The room that you have been elevated to is not of material substance, it is tranquil, within the energies.*

Here are some ideas for mentally crossing over from the material to the spiritual.

We've talked about sweet spots and frequencies before. The first task is to try to get on the same wavelength as your Spirit Guide. This means using your mind to lift your thoughts away from the material and the physical. The aim is to cleanse stresses and strains elsewhere in our consciousness, at least for a short time. Meditation can be a daily practice to help you unwind and not necessarily connect with Spirit. A daily meditation to de-stress at the start or end of your day begins to let the easing flow.

Whatever your intention, try this:

Sit in a comfortable, straight-backed chair with your feet

or. Close your eyes and concentrate on your
ancing your breathing is a proven way of calming
lled breathing sends a soothing, relaxing message
.

Regulate your breathing intake. Breathe in, hold and release. Breathe through your nose, count up to four, hold, then breathe out through your mouth to the count of five as your diaphragm expands and contracts. Do this about five times. With practice, your brain will remember this pattern and you'll slide into a wonderful meditative state.

*Tapping before meditating.*

Shedding stress is not easy. Here's an effective technique you can try. It's called Tapping or Emotional Freedom Technique (EFT). EFT is a way to use your fingertips to gently 'tap' on your energy points in your upper body. It's like acupuncture but without needles. This is a way to ease pressure and stress either before you meditate or to reduce nerves or anxieties if you're worried about anything or about to go for an interview or take an exam, for example.

Use your fingertips of either your left or right hands, to tap a soft rhythm. At the same time, you could either think them or say out loud, words of affirmation, of encouragement. Forget about stress, have confidence, or say hello to your higher self. Dispel negativity from your mind and body. It really does work. You gain a stillness that when you've finished, you will be re-energised.

This image shows the positions to tap. This is a recommended sequence from a professional coach. Tap each place for a few moments before moving on:

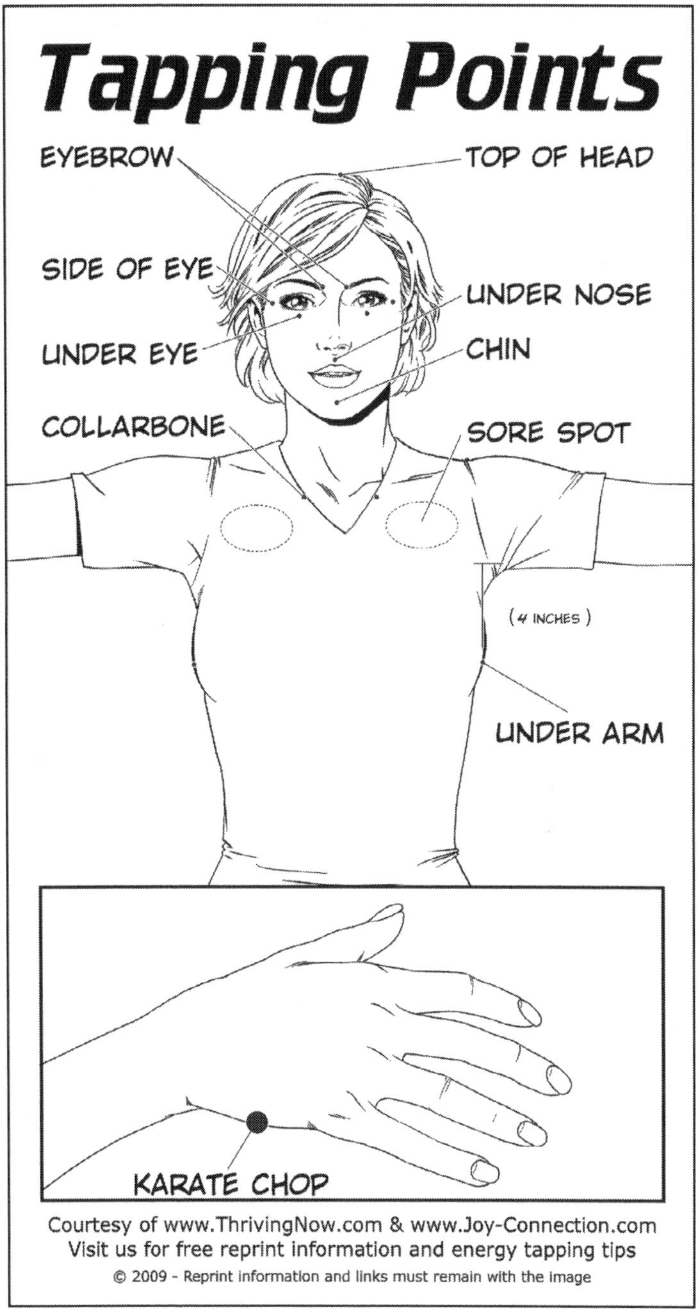
Tapping Points
EYEBROW
TOP OF HEAD
SIDE OF EYE
UNDER NOSE
UNDER EYE
CHIN
COLLARBONE
SORE SPOT
( 4 INCHES )
UNDER ARM
KARATE CHOP
Courtesy of www.ThrivingNow.com & www.Joy-Connection.com
Visit us for free reprint information and energy tapping tips
© 2009 - Reprint information and links must remain with the image

1. Tap on the side of your hand, as shown in the picture
2. Then slowly up tap your neck to the top of your head and tap on your crown
3. Tap in the centre of your eyebrows
4. Use both hands to tap by the side of your eyes
5. Then below your nose
6. The centre point of your chin
7. On your collarbone
8. The centre of your chest
9. On the point below your armpit
10. On the inside of your wrists near your pulse points
11. Tap gently on the top of your hands, behind the knuckles
12. Return to the side of your hands in the 'karate' chop position

As I was writing this piece, Grey Dove and Black Raven wanted to make a contribution on the theme of meditation. These are Grey Dove's words:

*If you are very new to this, not everybody who is meditating is for the sole purpose of connecting with the spiritual energies.*

*Many meditate because it calms their minds. I am going to give you some tips on how you can link with the spiritual energies or to your higher self. The most important thing is to be comfortable and place yourself in an environment where it is quiet and you cannot listen to the cars, planes or trains.*

*Sit in a place where it is not black but quite dark where it will suit you when you have your eyes closed. Where you sit is very important. You need to be comfortable in a chair, you need to be warm. Have you got a blanket or a wrap in case you get cold? You need to have water too. Once the preparation is done set aside a time when you can meditate and sit within the quietness.*

*When everything is settled, we go into the room. Shut the door and put your feet on the floor, don't have your legs crossed or you could stop the flow of the blood and you may get pins and needles and be uncomfortable and disturb the flow of thought and meditation.*

*Once you sit and relax, you can place your hands upon your knees. We come to the point where the mind is meant to be still. People will say that it is difficult for the mind to be still; if you go back centuries, people will still be saying it is difficult for the mind to be still. In this day and age, there is so much going on.*

*You've got your body still. You could put on light and soothing music to help still the mind. Imagine that the light is coming all around you. This light can be whatever shade you would like it to be. Blue, white, people automatically think of the white light being sent down from the realms. The light is there for protection. Whatever light you'd like it to be imagine the light is filling your whole body. Sit quietly and ask the energies all around you to still your body and your thoughts.*

I'm the last person to take issue with Grey Dove, but here goes.

He writes: 'Sit in a place where it is not black but quite dark where it will suit you when you have your eyes closed.' I agree with Suzi, who pointed out that you can meditate anywhere at any time, inside or outside the home. Just by closing your eyes, you can slip into a quiet, restorative, meditative state. Forgive me, Grey Dove.

Black Raven joined us during the same meeting on 30 March 2023.

*Once you're comfortable, let your mind drift.*

*I thought you may like some pointers of how people can meditate in a soft and comfortable environment. This is my tip to you, my friend.*

*The art of meditation is to connect with your higher self. Not to step outside your body but to concentrate on the energy you can create yourself. The whole point is to gain that stillness within yourself, to alleviate any stresses and anxieties you may have. People, like my fellow energy friend Grey Dove has just said, you are speaking to Raven.*

*When Canuji converses with people he often tells people to imagine that he is a Black Panther and that the Black Panther can bring strength and energy and bring those healing gifts that he possesses.*

*When you hear my voice, my friend, I would just think of a black raven with yellow eyes. It's not there to frighten or scare. It is a bird of prey, a bird of protection, when they stretch their wings, they see far and appear larger than they actually are. The spiritual Raven, the spiritual me, is there for healing, and meditation, that is there for healing.*

*Many people do not put the two together. People meditate for different reasons. You will have the monks who meditate to become one with their gods, to become one with their higher self. You have people who are in their circles who are trying to connect with the spiritual realms. They meditate in the hope that their guides will come to them. If they come, they will give them messages and will be able to start to talk and give them the okay to walk along the pathway of Spirit. People do not always understand what it is like to go into pure meditation where you are healing yourself from inside out. As my fellow energy friend said, it is preparation that's important. It does not matter what your purposes are for meditation you have to get the preparation right. If you sit in the quiet and darkness, the soothing energy will help you.*

*People like to mediate as well if they have ailments. If they meditate, they will help the ailments. It's like self-healing that comes from within. Imagine that your mind is there no longer. It is projecting your energy to protect your own body. It's reaching out to reach your higher self to make that connection with the realms. They know their physicality is linked with the earth and they are still going along doing their daily business. There are many ways to meditate, some people like to lie down, some to sit. Some like to make noises with chanting 'OM', to get that negativity out of themselves. Whether you believe in the spiritual realms or not, my friend, it is for one sole reason it is to still their mind, quieten their mind and try to give themselves self-healing. It is something like a job of work, my friend. If you do just one session or two sessions you will not get much out of it.*

*If you do it on a regular basis, it becomes very important. It is like booking an appointment with Spirit. Some people think that they can connect with Spirit anytime they want. However, the spiritual energies like to have regularity and punctuality. It does not mean, my friend, that if you are late or not regular, we are going to remove our energies, that would not happen. Regularity and punctuality are important in your world and our world.*

*We are here at any time to answer any questions you may have in your mind and we know at times you may know the answers but also that you like to embellish what has been given to you.*

The Tree of Life Meditation is a powerful one to try.

### *The Tree of Life Meditation*

The Tree of Life is an ancient symbol of immortality. The roots entwining with the branches of the tree creates one continuous circular link. They make the eternal connection between Heaven and Earth. The Tree of Life can be the inspiration for a powerful meditation exercise to raise the earth's magnetic force upward and draw down the Divine light from above.

Visualisation:

- Sit comfortably on a chair without shoes or you can lie flat on the floor. Rest your hands on your thighs. Gently roll your shoulders and move your head and neck from side to side to release any muscular tension.
- Close your eyes. Direct all your mental energy to your feet. Imagine you are as one with the earth. Visualise small tree roots sprouting from the soles of your feet and tiny roots stemming from your toes.
- See the roots burrowing through the floor, driving down, piercing the foundations of your house, going deeper and deeper into the soil, past rocks and stones penetrating to the centre of the earth.
- All the while, the roots are growing bigger and stronger drawing up earth's magnetic energy.
- Energy travels upwards through your roots like streams of molten lava. You look down. Your ankles, calves and legs have joined to form the single trunk of the tree. Bark crackles and forms a protective layer as your tree trunk widens through your hips, getting thicker and taller, going higher and higher, leaving the ground way below you.
- Look upwards. Your shoulders and arms have sprouted a thousand branches. Leaves have created a gloriously

green canopy above you. You see a beam of dazzling light moving like a lightning strike through the canopy and down the trunk, to blend seamlessly with earth's magnetic energy rising upwards along your trunk to meet at your solar plexus, the heart centre of your being.

- Hold that image. Feel the spiritual energy pulse through your body. Stay in the moment for as long as you wish. Slowly, open your eyes. Come back. Relaxed.

## Blog

*The Power of Thought Energy*

Our minds are powerhouses of energy. Thought waves generated by our minds are transmitters and receptors of Spirit. The energy of thought creates channels of communication, invisible tendrils of understanding that spark our minds and stimulate our senses. This can be a physical sensation, as if you're feeling electrical static over your head and fluffing with your hair or feeling a gentle puff of air across your cheek as if a breath is being softly blown in your direction. These are calling signs to let you know Spirit is with you.

What's faster than the speed of light? It is the speed of thought. Think it and it happens. Bring something to mind and it takes solid form in your head in an instant. Memories are recaptured and replayed; they're brought front and centre in your mind. They live again. The energy of thought is indestructible, as your Spirit and soul are indestructible. When our time on earth has run its course, it is our spiritual energy that survives; our consciousness survives as energy. Thought is the vehicle that creates a reality around us. We become spheres of energy in a world of love and peace. These are the words of a Spirit Guide on the power of thought:

> *Imagine you have no body; your eyes are closed and you are floating in the air. All around you is extreme peace and you feel no weight at all. Suddenly you want to walk, to place your feet upon the floor. There is no floor, you are in the air. You put your arms out to help you stand. There is nothing for you to hold on to. You're in nothingness.*
>
> *This is an example to help you understand how you would automatically open your eyes and immediately come back to the physical. By engaging your imagination, the mind, you would still be able to walk, talk, run, jump, dance, sing, and continue to 'do' whatever you could do on earth.*
>
> *You will hear many stories of information from a departed Spirit who would have been paralysed when on the earth, saying to their loved ones that my legs and arms are working perfectly well now. I can straighten my back; I could even do somersaults if so desired. The blind person would say they can see perfectly clearly now, the deaf person would say they can now hear clearly. The mute person would be able to talk. The imperfections of the body have been left behind and they are now operating only with crystal clarity from the power of thought.*

The spiritual world runs on thought energy powered by the divine light.

## Coming Next

### *Mediumship*

In the next chapter, we'll cover the subject of Mediumship. You will learn about the main forms, and Janet will pass on her tips if you decide to develop these skills yourself.

# Four

## Mediumship

*Messengers of Spirit*

Mediumship is the practical connection between humanity and spiritual energies. Mediumship is the psychic affirmation that the spiritual world exists.

It is only when you experience the excitement of hearing evidence for yourself from those you have loved and lost that you begin to believe. It is personal evidence that convinces.

Everyone has an innate psychic ability to develop their spiritual talents. In *Believe in Spirit* we described the various forms of psychic awareness stemming from the French word *clair* meaning 'clear'. Here they are again.

## *Four Invisible Gifts of Intuition*

Intuition is immensely powerful. We draw upon it when we instinctively sense something. Our minds send alert signals to our consciousness. This is where the Four Gifts of Intuition come in. They are part of our range of spiritual skills. A Spiritual Medium would have developed these gifts to be able to connect with Spirit when they act as a communication channel between our two worlds.

A description of Spiritual Mediums and Mediumship:

### *1. Clairvoyance*

'Clear-seeing' is when images are visualised in the mind. For a Spiritual Medium, clear-seeing is the ability, with expert training, to visualise and describe the departed spirits who wish to make contact with their loved ones. A description would normally relate to the way the Spirit looked in terms of height, weight, visual appearance, hair colour, clothing but also pick up on points of their character, moods and personality. Sometimes the way they spoke, things they said and how they said it would confirm someone's identity.

Additionally, evidence may involve the way a person passed into Spirit, for example, natural causes, in a car or motorcycle accident, or through cancer or other medical condition. The Medium could see or get a sense of the trauma involved. Not to cause distress but to provide evidence that spiritual life continues. The searing pain of losing them will be eased knowing that they are safe. After a Spirit passes, they are surrounded by love and peace, without stress, without pain. Getting that confirmation will let you know for certain that they will forever be alive to help and guide you. They will always be a single thought away.

It is important that clairvoyant readings provide evidential support of the information given by a Medium. This can be at the time of the message or corroborated later when something comes to light to prove the accuracy of what has been given. This is referred to as evidential clairvoyance.

These are the words of Archangel Michael on the work of Mediums:

> *Understanding is the most important thing. We want people who do the work to be proud of themselves for bringing loved ones through, to make people happy or make them cry tears of happiness. But they may not have the understanding of what they are doing, of who they are working with. They may know they give out the messages as it is an important thing. But, the most important thing is to understand the spiritual world, and the energies and to understand how you have said it and that you are Spirit in a physical body.*

To bring this explanation to life, I asked three practising Spiritual Mediums, as well as Janet, to describe what it's like for them when they connect with Spirit to deliver clairvoyant messages. My thanks to Rosie, Isabelle and Suzi.

This was Isabelle's reply:

*The connection usually starts with me seeing in part or a whole picture, as if I'm watching a film or looking at a photo and as it slowly reveals itself. I get a sense of the person and sometimes hear words as well but generally, it is a 'knowing' and information that is impressed into my mind.*

Rosie said this:

*I can confirm that I often see Spirit. I used to see them like flesh, but now it's either in my mind's eye or mostly as mist, like a wisp of smoke, but then it's the whole person that takes shape.*

*When I do the Soul Rescue, they often appear in the mind's eye to begin with, then mist/smoke and then build up to flesh in most cases.*

Author Note: We'll be introducing you to Soul Rescue in Chapter Ten.

And Suzi:

*For me, connecting with Spirit is when I get a pull in my solar plexus as I am about to start to work. Then I know someone's there. Once this happens, I'm pulled towards a person as I look round the congregation. I feel like being physically moved from one end of the raised platform to the other. (To locate the person who will receive the message.)*

*I don't see a light over anybody or anything like that. I don't see anything and I don't hear anything either. I have this pulling sensation. I open my mouth and Spirit directs my speaking.*

*I help the flow by first saying something like, 'Okay, I have someone here and I'd like to go to the lady over there…' Then off we go! I feel the emotions and can take on characteristics of the Spirit person as they were in life (and still are!) to pass on their message.*

Here's Janet's description of the clairvoyance experience:

*When working to pass on clairvoyant messages, for me, it's not hearing a voice or seeing visions or people, it's a flow of energy from Spirit straight into my aura. Within that flow of energy is all the information that's needed to be passed onto the sitter. It's very much a two-way link from Spirit to myself. Also within that flow of energy is the ability for me to see, not with clarity how people would expect but with the description of visions.*

*Every word which is uttered by myself is exactly how it has been passed on by the energy within that flow of energy, the only words changed are those of colourful language. It is the union between Spirit and myself that has enabled the link between us to flow fluidly.*

*Once the energy is flowing between myself and Spirit, that is when the energy who is making connection come alive, their personality and mannerisms are very much there as if they were in the room. They talk about themselves exactly how they would have been upon the earth, warts and all. Within the communication, their sense of humour can become very lively and at other times their emotions can cause many tears to flow.*

Here's an introduction to three other gifts of intuition.

*2. Clairsentient*

'Clear-feeling' is linked to the sense of touch or feeling. It's when you're sensitive to intuitive sensations from the mind. This may be linked to feelings that are linked with the manner of their passing. A Spiritual Medium may feel a similar pain in their chest to suggest someone died of a heart attack, or they may begin to cough or feel a rasping in the chest if the departed Spirit suffered from a respiratory problem. The scent of perfume, tobacco smoke or alcohol or other distinctive smells could be sensed by a Medium during a reading. All these could paint a vivid picture in the mind; the smell of the ocean, the tang of salt spray, any of these could trigger a memory that is significant.

*3. Clairaudience*

'Clear-hearing' stems from within the mind of the Medium. Voices, words, sounds, or musical tunes or instruments are sensed. This could happen as part of a spiritual reading when a Medium asks the departed Spirit for more information or clarification. The Medium would tune in to listen to the voice of the person in Spirit.

*4. Claircognisence*

'Clear-knowing' comes from the root word cognitive, which relates to knowledge, learning and understanding. In psychic terms it links to the immediate intuitive sense, the mental and physical perception that's a spiritual experience. It is also linked with premonitions, where a feeling is a signal of something that's about to happen. This can be either good or bad and can relate to an event to a person, in nature or a disastrous occurrence.

### *Blending Gifts*

Any one of these gifts could dominate. However, it is more likely they would blend in levels of sensitivity for someone. Interestingly, the thing is that three of the 'Claires', clairsentience, clairaudience and claircognisence, can be signs of extra psychic sensitivity without necessarily leading to clairvoyance and developing a 'seeing' link with Spirit or of taking a spiritual direction. They may stand alone as psychic gifts.

### *Where Could You Go from Here?*

You could visit a spiritual church to witness a Medium connecting with Spirit. The atmosphere is relaxed and welcoming. It is not religiously formal. By the way, instead of using the word 'church', often these places are described as spiritual centres or sanctuaries. Inside, they differ from conventional churches. There's a raised platform where an altar would be. This is where services are conducted from and where Mediums stand to be seen by the congregation.

In the UK, there's a Divine Service on a Sunday morning or evening. The service includes a healing prayer, an inspirational reading, an address on a spiritual topic followed by a demonstration of clairvoyance that would last for about half an hour. A longer demonstration of clairvoyance takes place one evening during the week, usually on a Monday or Wednesday.

There are free-will offerings for people to give whatever they can afford. There is an unwritten code in public meetings to never reveal private information. More personal information may be given during private readings. A thread of care, of love and respect, runs through everything.

Spiritual Healing is held during the daytime or after one of the evening events. These are open to everyone. Private readings with a Medium are also arranged to raise funds to keep the doors open. During services, Mediums are expected to connect clairvoyantly with their Spirit Guides to provide messages from loved ones of a spiritual nature.

To explain, Mediums can work psychically as well as spiritually. Working psychically, a Medium is not passing on messages direct from their guides and in the main, not from loved ones in Spirit. Here, the focus is on personal matters. A Medium can sense the mood, appearance and demeanour of a person. They can get an understanding from their aura about their state of mind. These intuitive triggers give a reading which reflects their material and mental state at a particular moment in time. An assessment can be made about their emotional, material and physical well-being. Finance, relationships, employment, health, these are everyday pressures in our lives. These are helpful, practical, private insights.

## *Joining a Circle*

Another option in exploring and developing your spiritual self is to join a circle. People of all ages meet to learn from experienced Mediums. The first group is termed an 'open' circle, which attracts those who want to see if this is for them. This is often a starting point. It will be a gentle introduction to relaxation and meditation techniques. Being made aware of your chakras and energy centres of your body will be one strand of learning, as well as practising techniques to stimulate your psychic awareness. You'll meet new friends of like mind. You would be encouraged to attend on a regular basis but that decision is yours alone. No pressure.

A 'closed' circle is where members have made their own commitment to develop their individual skills over time with help and support. This is when you've made a decision to devote your energy to the learning process. Every person progresses at their own pace. It will take time for you to become in sync with your guide. They will be with you at every step you take.

### *Notes on Circles*

If you're thinking of becoming a Medium, here are some pointers from Janet:

Developing to become a Medium isn't always as easy as you might imagine. There is a saying, 'We only get out of things what we put in.' This is true for so many things we do within our lifetimes, especially Mediumship.

We all develop at different times and stages. Never compare yourself to anyone else, we're all on our own personal, unique pathway.

### *Dedication. Punctuality. Regularity*

These are the main thoughts that are important when joining a circle:

### *Dedication*

When your mind is fixed on to learning something new; there's a feeling within us that we want to succeed now, straight away, in an instant.

Developing to become a Medium is rarely like that. It can be a very slow process. It takes time and patience, not a few weeks or a couple of months, it may take years to get to where you feel ready to pass on those all-important messages of proof of life in the hereafter.

We never stop learning and developing. This is why it's important to maintain the dedication we first experience at the beginning of the journey. To dedicate your time and thoughts is very important, not just at the beginning but all the way through.

This does not mean to say you have to stop any other hobbies or activities. It's always important to have something else completely different in your life. Even if this means switching off by reading novels, listening to music, playing an instrument, gardening or going for walks. These can be good ways of clearing your mind from slowly being aware of loving energies around you. Especially when your guides are blending their energies with your own. It can become intense at times and it's good to have something else to take your mind away. This mental break will help you continue on your journey.

### *Punctuality*

When attending meetings for the circle, always be punctual. In a circle, there will be a time set by the leader of the group. It's important to arrive maybe five or ten minutes before the circle starts. This will be in order for everyone to settle down and quieten their minds away from daily pressures. Lateness can cause disharmony. Remember, when sitting in a group, you all have to work together. This is important for the energies of the circle members to blend.

### *Regularity*

Always try to attend regularly for the meetings. It's important for your development. At times, when holidays or illness intervene, missing a meeting can't be avoided. Being committed and attending regularly is acknowledged and appreciated by your guide. It's a matter of respect.

If you intend to develop on your own without joining a circle, or if you form a separate group of like-minded people, set aside a particular time and stick to it on a regular basis.

It may surprise you but Spirit also like to be punctual and regular with the meetings. Some people run away with the thought that we can conjure up the spiritual energies whenever we want. But in a teaching situation it is like joining a classroom to learn your lessons. There needs to be a structure to follow and respect. You will find, especially at the beginning of your journey, that spiritual energies, just like yourself, are learning and developing alongside you. This means it's important for both parties to be as regular and punctual as possible.

A few tips about passing on messages:

When talking to someone you would normally make eye contact. When a Medium has connected to Spirit, the Medium should try *not* to look directly at the sitter but look at a space above the sitter's head or over their shoulders. Not at their face or into their eyes. You see, Mediumship is about energy. That's how the link is formed. Energy is delivered from Spirit to the

Medium, who in turn, passes on the message. The Medium could be distracted by positive or negative facial expressions or sounds or words made by the sitter. The sitter's energy could be distracting and cause static interference.

The main reason for delivering messages is to give the proof that their loved ones or friends are still very much alive in mind, thought and energy. It's common practice in Mediumship that after a Medium has given solid proof of the continued existence of the friend or relative, to deliver a message from their loved one to the sitter.

These messages are given directly from Spirit and are not meant to be changed in any way. Avoiding eye contact with the sitter will keep the message exactly how it is meant to be. It's an easy mistake to make. If you link with the sitter, you'll find yourself reading them rather than passing on the message accurately from Spirit.

My guides have three golden rules when delivering messages:

- Never give bad news.
- Never give someone's personal business away.
- Never intentionally embarrass anyone.

There's no point in passing on any of these. The whole point of making contact with the afterlife is that they go away with a sense of relief that their loved ones in Spirit are happy and at peace.

As time passes, your spiritual awareness expands.

This increased understanding may lead to developing an aptitude that builds upon the Four Gifts of Intuition. Your spirituality and your personal expression of Mediumship can also expand through the gift of healing or include an ability to communicate using the written or spoken word. These help to raise awareness of the existence and role of Spirit in our lives. To Spirit, anyone who works with them to shine their love and learning can be thought of as a Medium. Spirit takes us on different pathways to suit our innate abilities and spiritual nature. Healing and Soul Rescue are two such examples. These will flow in the pages to follow.

### *Channelling: Another Level of Mediumship*

You've read that clairvoyance has the supremely important role of providing evidence that life continues after physical death. Mediums reconnect with friends and loved ones who have passed into Spirit. There is another level called channelling where Mediums connect directly with their Spirit Guides and converse with them.

A Medium will willingly enter an altered state of consciousness to form this link between their energy and their guides. Trust and belief grow over time to achieve this heightened state of consciousness. To an observer this could seem as though the Medium is entranced. This has led to the word Trance being used to describe the process. The Medium is not hypnotised nor controlled. The Medium participates of their own free will. The depth of the experience is immensely rewarding. It transcends the Medium to reach a higher level of awareness and understanding.

We've given you an insight into what it's like for a Medium to work clairvoyantly, what they feel and what they transmit to others. Janet, Suzi, Gilly and Michael channel. The sensation is different when they channel. This is Suzi's description:

*I don't see anything. They just speak their description through me. It's like I am taken over, but lightly. Except when there is a strong point they want to make. Then I can sense that the energy is really powerful, especially if they are used to taking centre stage.*

*Everything I do, they speak it through me. I literally just open my mouth. My job is to get out of the way, and that is what it feels like. That understanding is what sitting for weeks, months and years in development circles is all about. And to learn to trust and be safe. I can't reiterate that enough. It really does feel like they are taking charge of my body with certain hand or arm movements to express themselves but never 'taken over'.*

*At first, I used to get scared by it all, but now it just feels natural; it's so important to be with people where you feel safe when developing. The Trance started immediately for me, that's how they came through in the very beginning. People in the know sometimes say to me they can tell I'm a Trance Medium, people in the audience who know about it.*

Janet added her experience:

*When working in trance or channelling, at the very beginning it felt as if my body was being taken over entirely, as if an energy was all over me. I realise now that this was because when working in this capacity the energies are blending at a much more forceful way; therefore, it takes more time and patience to adjust to the changes that are happening.*

*It is completely different energy-wise when you are working clairvoyantly, it's much gentler.*

*Now it's much easier because over a long period of time the energies of myself and Spirit have become more compatible with one another. The energy feels heavier and that is because the energy from Spirit draws much nearer and deeper into my own energy field.*

*Whatever way you are working, there is one thing that we all have to take into consideration and that is our development and progress depends on how much time, dedication and patience we put in. Working alongside the Spirit energies takes time. It's not in anyone's interest to rush the process; this will only hinder your development. Also, remember to enjoy the journey.*

### *How Does This Work?*

The two energies meld together to sensitively, emotionally, and trustingly combine. Spirit use their Medium's vocal cords to speak their words.

Often the guides introduce themselves with their given names during their earthly lifetime. We also recognise them by the way they speak, the subjects they raise, and the tone of their voices. Female guides tend to have lighter, softer voices. Their personalities shine through. They talk about the lives they led. Their stories are full of drama, sorrow and joy. Just like ours. We love to hear about their time on earth.

Let's share some of these interactions with you. This conversation is from Grey Dove, a Native American Indian.

He regularly takes part in our meetings. Here is one of his messages received on Friday, 17 March 2023. He mentions the Mediumistic gifts of intuition.

From Grey Dove:

*Good day, my friend. There's a saying in your world that God is there in each and every one of you. He lives and breathes in everyone. There is another saying that God maps out your lives. We have said this many times. Or is it in the preparation before you go back to the earth? Because, my friend, there is preparation before you return to earth when you are still in the spiritual realms.*

*There is a whole world that is invisible to the naked eye. It is dense energy that is full of the energy of mind and thought. If you could see it in your mind's eye this is how people make connections with the power of mind and thought. It is possible through their own mind's eye for them to see images of the energy they have. This is the power of thought. It is so powerful that you can create these images within your mind. It is called clairvoyance, clairsentience, clairaudience, everything that people like to picture and explain to other people so they know how it all works, how it all functions.*

*Within our world it is like looking up to the sky, it is full of grey clouds but if you could imagine, that would be a mass of dense energy. That is made up of tiny individual dots of energy that is the spiritual energies. So therefore, each and every one of them is very much alive.*

*I want to backtrack and say that is not how our world looks, not as a mass dense of cloud but that's the only way I can explain it to you so you can get a picture of how we are. Within this mass of dense energy, people can also have the power to link in and connect and see energies. If you come back to the spiritual realms, your journey begins as this new Spirit coming back but your journey has already begun as if you have already been reincarnated within another physical incarnation. It is like walking side by side with the string of your other energies. Does this make sense to you? It's like walking along a ladder and another ladder next to it. The first ladder would have many rungs and go up high. Another ladder would be halfway up. Do you get the gist of what I'm saying?*

*Therefore, it's a new journey for that new Spirit who has just returned but it is an old journey where everything comes together and you know within the power of thought, exactly what pathway you want to go on. There are many options, my friend. You can continue going up and up to the spiritual realms through as many levels as you want. You can learn, you can keep learning all the knowledge until you eventually pass that knowledge down to the people on the earth if you wish to do so.*

*It is not all about gaining the knowledge then passing it back to people in human form. It's about learning knowledge so you can pass it on to other energies within the spiritual realms who so wish to be a part of the human life. Does this make sense? It is like where the Halls of Learning come into play as not every energy that is in the Halls of Learning are kept for the future as they have done for the past. They are focussing on the future. Not ten years or twenty or thirty years, but far, far in the future. It is all set there as it takes a long time for this knowledge to be filtered down to the earth. This is where my part, my friend, becomes interesting. Part of the information that is within the Halls of Learning for the future will be directed into the spiritual energies that will be filtered into energies who are back within the realms whose thoughts and ideas are to do with having another journey within an incarnated body. Spiritual energies don't put their hands up or get in a queue and say, 'I want to do this.' They are chosen at random, any spiritual energy that is at some point going to make the preparations to go back to earth again. It is to put back that theme of excellence within their minds to plant the seed, not of power but that seed of what they really wish to embellish upon.*

*When it is their time to go back to the earth, it doesn't matter, my friend, of how their lives start, whether they are privileged or underprivileged, once that thought is there, that gift is bedded within their mind, they will make it, whatever they do as it will come to the forefront of their minds. Once again, my friend, I am being interrupted by another energy who feels it is in their best interest to explain this better than I am. You see it is exactly the same as in the realms as on the earth plane. If we were on the earth plane, we would consider it very rude but within the spiritual realms we still consider it rude but we allow the intervene. My friend, you have been speaking to Grey Dove or rather you have been listening to Grey Dove as he has been doing all the talking. I am now going to be mute and see whether my friend wishes to embellish on what I've been saying.*

Before we leave the subject of Mediumship, I wanted to check something with Janet. At times, when I'm writing, Janet makes contact with her principal guide to answer any queries. Here's one example:

'Janet, can you ask Running Water a question? Do Mediums who are linked with different faith groups; do they connect with guides who are linked with their own religious beliefs? What I mean is, do Hindu Mediums or other Holy Men and Women; do they get their messages from Spirit in the form of Hindu Gods or Sikh or Islamic teachers, for example?'

Running Water answered:

> *When connecting with Spirit, one's subconscious mind will automatically gravitate towards energies of a like-mind. However, once in Spirit, belief systems change. They are all joined as one. The religious differences are only for the earth. Many Mediums have guides or helpers who would have followed different pathways. The whole belief system becomes universal when in Spirit.*

Followers of different faiths visualise images linked with their belief on this side of life. That explains the Christian tradition with the writers of this book and our respectful spiritual oneness with other faith groups.

A note. In our books we've focused on mainstream Mediumship. There are other avenues known as physical Mediumship you may wish to explore.

# Blog

*Evidence of Everlasting Life*

The primary duty of a Spiritual Medium is to prove that life continues after physical death.

It is their duty to pass on the love from friends and family who are no longer here. Their Spirit still lives. They may not be in the material world but they still exist in mind, thought and energy. The moment you think of a loved one they come alive in your head. The question is, how can someone who you don't know provide the kind of proof your heart yearns for? What kind of evidence can they supply to convince you? What will it take for you to feel that divine surge of understanding and experience that sublime revelation when they do connect with a loved one?

We all have psychic ability. It is that invisible source of deepest thought energy from our minds. Many of us never tap into this ability. It lays dormant, undiscovered. Often the only hint we have is when our intuition triggers an idea in our heads or we get a twinge in our gut. A Spiritual Medium has often gone through years of training to accept, embrace and link their spirituality together with their Spirit Guide.

The process connects our two worlds; it is a blending of mind energy. Simply put, the Medium performs the role of communicator, the go-between. They accept and direct messages from Spirit. Spirit makes contact when they want to speak to us. A Medium cannot decide to make contact as if they are making a person-to-person call. Spirit controls the communication exchange; they make the first move. Deceased spirits make contact with their Spirit Guide using their thought energy when they want to pass on a message to someone on Earth.

This is when the earth contact is made. Imagine a church service and you are a member of the congregation. We each have our own spiritual light that emanates from our aura and shines from the top of our heads. That's what Spirit sees. The brighter the light, the more spiritual you are. The Medium senses or sees your light in their minds. The role of the Medium is to first identify the deceased Spirit-side who wants to communicate with someone quietly sitting and suspecting nothing in the church service until they're about to receive a message. It often comes as a big surprise.

Often the sequence begins with the Medium saying what relation – friend or family – they are to you. This may be followed by a physical description of them when they were living here. The clothes they wore, the way they walked, their height and weight, perhaps their name. More information follows, perhaps about their personality, the type of person they were and how you interacted with them. As this information flows, the Medium will check with you to see if you recognise the deceased person in Spirit. They will want to hear your voice, as this is important to create and maintain contact across the ether.

When you realise who has 'come through', a personal message is usually given. The message concerns your spiritual self. It's not fortune telling, it is about aspects of your life to prove that they know you and want to send love and guidance.

Clairvoyance provides evidence that the deceased are alive in Spirit, watching over and caring for you. Think of it as speaking to your extended family on the other side of life.

## Coming Next

*Conversations with Spirit*

Over the years, Janet has helped newcomers to Mediumship develop their talents in her weekly circles. In parallel, she's had the wonderful experience of working with some exceptional Mediums who've joined her advanced channelling sessions. These include Gilly, Cindy, Suzi, and more recently, Michael.

Chapter Five is devoted to conversations with Spirit that could challenge everything you thought you knew. They've been recorded and written down, word for word.

# Five

## Conversations with Spirit

How do you describe conversations between two worlds? The joy of channelling is to be able to speak to and react with spiritual energies. We speak as friends. Conversations happen over time and space. These exchanges are overwhelming in their magnificence. In the beginning, they seem beyond our comprehension. You cannot believe they're happening. And yet they do.

We never know what is going to happen. Who will make contact, what they want to say, how many guides will join the session or how long it will last for. The meetings are hosted by Running Water, Janet's Navajo Indian guide. He acts as gatekeeper on the Spirit side and gives permission for energies to speak to us using Janet's vocal cords.

On the earth side, the meetings comprise Janet, me and one perhaps two other guest Mediums who join the interaction with their personal guides speaking through their vocal cords. The guides never cease to amaze. The messages you are about to read show how deep their love is for us. They sense our state of mind. They're aware of the concerns we have and the issues in our personal lives and the state of the world around us. They encourage us. They feel for us. They understand the challenges we face in this mortal life.

We've chosen a number of transcripts at random. These are from the many meetings we've had to give an insight into one of the most staggering experiences imaginable. We'll begin with a meeting held in the New Year 2023.

*7 January 2023*

Janet and Steve, Saturday morning meeting. Running Water opens the conversation. His words are recorded on an iPad.

> *People all over the world are celebrating New Year and wish for more light in the New Year. People take the opportunity and the time to brush off the old and embrace the new and move forward. Many people have great expectations when*

*the new year begins. Some think that time ticks away with nothing special, another day dawns, another sunset comes. At the beginning of your new year, we do not speak to you personally but to the people who live in this world. People rejoice as they see out the old year and welcome in the new. People make New Year resolutions but rarely do they keep them. It is something they start to focus on and they have well-meaning lives that set in and intervene. We have spoken to you about time before and how time is relentless. This is what we want to speak to you about today. Some people are afraid of time, the clock is ticking away, and time goes very quickly.*

*What we want to say to you, Stephen, is that we do not want you to focus on time. We want you to focus on yourself and how you can get things done. There is no time limit. We do not want you to rush or feel that you are within a time bracket where you have to get certain things done. With your writings, they will get done when the time is right.*

A different energy joins the conversation.

*Good day, my friends. It is a privilege to come through again and converse with you, as we like to speak to you and learn your thoughts. We do not need to hear your thoughts verbally. We can go through your minds and the mind of the energy we are tapping into. We know this is weighing heavily upon you. There is a saying on your earth that time waits for no man, and it is true. Time is no importance as if you rush things, they will have to be done again and so you are waiting. My friend, you have plenty of time left on the earth, you're not going anywhere soon. There's no point in us working all our energies on both your energies to bring you over here very quickly, so all the work that we want you to do, we would have to seek out other energies to do that. My friend, we are very happy with the energies we have chosen. So, for the foreseeable future you will be both on the earth to work and liaise together.*

*There's no rush to get the words down. We want you to do it in your own time and be relaxed. We don't want you to be uptight, anxious or distressed. If you start to write down the words that don't flow freely, you will have to change them again because they will not be in the right context, and everything has to be in the right context. My friend, those are things I wanted to say to you but now I'm going to pick up on what Running Water was saying.*

*It is the dawning of another New Year and another episode in everyone's life. People have great expectations at the beginning of a new year because they feel the old has gone behind them and any mistakes they made in the old year can be rectified in the new year. First of all, we know what ails you and it will get sorted out then you will start to feel a lot easier in your mind. This is what is holding you back even though you are determined to continue your writings.*

*Now I want to change the subject, as I want to talk about your universe as a whole, not just the country or land that you reside, as everybody, every country, has their own choices to make on how they view their country and the mistakes that everyone is making.*

*The universe is a vast area indeed, as you know, and there are many planets. We speak of your world that is spinning around on its axis. People are destroying the world and destroying your planet. Think about this, my friend; this is the result of progression. Over the years, hundreds of years, people are developing and coming up with new ways of how to move forward with materials and everything else you use. It is some of these methods and machinery that are destroying the habitat. It is done without realising what is happening. Thankfully, people are trying to pinpoint the mistakes in what they are doing. Everyone has to try to undo the damage that has been done. People are trying hard. They talk about your climate change and the way the earth is going. We want people to know that it is going to be a long hard work-in-progress in front of you all to get the earth back together.*

*The manufacturers need to up their game and change certain things. They could go back to their old material of what they were using. It is all these cheaper materials that are destroying the planet and the birdlife and fish in the oceans. If they go back to the older materials that do not cause the damage and the harm. On the earth, you are mixed up with all the negative energy. Positivity is light. Negativity is dark, it brings out the dark moods in people. If you put colours on everything, you can feel the lightness according to the colour. The colours blue and green are for healing, they are of the earth as the sky is blue and the sea is blue. The grass and the vegetation and trees are green and they come from the earth. It is like Spirit joining together. Also, you have the mauve and the colours of the rainbow with the chakras. If you get the greys and the blacks you do not feel happy. Grey makes you feel gloomy, black makes you feel dark. People associate negative energy with black and grey. When you come up the scale, you'll feel lighter. As you take the colour yellow, the colour of the sun. When the sun comes out, you instantly feel happy. Yellow and orange are happy colours. You have all the different colours and shades of blue and green. Pink is the colour of love, and people associate pink with happiness. Red is fire and danger and mixed with harmony. I wanted to mention about the colours as they are important. Colour can affect your health and well-being.*

*You have been listening to the words of an energy who is not very familiar to you, my friend. Thank you. My name will come at another time.*

Sister Theresa introduces herself as Christina, it was her birth name before she entered the convent. She joins the meeting:

*Good morning, it's Christina. I've come through but I've no idea how this conversation is going to go. I'm here and I find I can use my words. I just wanted to say that the topic of today has been the New Year. Other countries have their New Year at different times. It is more important for you to celebrate your New Year when the clock ticks loudly or the candle goes down very quickly. You look at it at one point and it would go down and clock ticks away. Sometimes people need a rest for themselves and shrug off that melancholy mood and do things that please you rather than do things that make sense.*

*It's very important to get that time right. So many people on the earth feel they should be doing things because they must do them either for themselves or for other people. It's something they have to do because they feel they should. I'm not talking about having to go to work. Sometimes you have to put these things in an order that would be more suitable rather than a drudge. Am I making sense? I'm not speaking to you at this moment in time but I know you can resonate with what I'm saying. Sometimes you feel as though you are on a bicycle and the wheels are locked with you peddling and peddling but not getting anywhere fast. You don't take yourself off the seat of the bicycle as you've got to keep going. That's until you take the brakes off and feel free. I think that's a good analogy of the way you are feeling.*

*I know that Black Feathers spoke about all the things that are going on in your mind. I want you to rest and relax, Stephen. As that is the best philosophy, as the focus will become clearer as you let your mind rest and relax. Otherwise, the focus is blurry and cloudy. You are still peddling on but you are not getting anywhere fast. You are just wearing yourself out. If you can focus and relax, everything will become clearer, lighter and brighter, and things will evolve in a clearer and better way. I hope that makes sense to you.*

*Running Water has just said, 'Christina, we are going to bring the meeting to an end. And because you're the last one, you can do the prayer.'*

Christina begins the closing prayer:

*I'm asking you to relax and focus on the colour you feel*

*brighter and lighter. As the Spirit said, the importance of the colour is far greater than people realise. I will put that colour mauve in your mind, as it is for healing and relaxation. It is the indigo associated within your auric field and spiritual realms.*

*I'm going to ask our dear Lord to bring this meeting to an end; that all the energy and light from the brightness of the spiritual realms has been absorbed by the people who are present within this building. And I ask the dear Lord, the dear God, to forgive everyone's sins they have committed, even if those sins are small so you can learn the rights and wrongs of life. If you do wrong within yourself it is not always a sin, but you learn from it. I would ask you to walk forward in a happier frame of mind.*

*From our world to yours, I leave you with all the love, tranquillity and peace that we can possibly bring. Amen.*

*6 January 2023*

*Black Feathers*

A few days later, Black Feathers, a member of the original Group of Eight Native American Indian Guides who instigated the first *Being Spirit* writing project back in 2018, wanted to talk about the changes and challenges a new year could bring.

*There comes a time in a person's life where changes are made, sometimes these changes are inevitable, they go along with the twists and turns in a person's pathway and at times can be hard to accept and adjust to; they then become challenging.*

*There is a saying upon your earth that your lives are mapped out for you from the onset of birth. In a small way there is some truth in this phrase. When the Spirit is still within the realms and are going through the adjustments and preparation for a new incarnation, it's set within their thoughts of how the thread of their lifetime will run. Once the return to earth has happened, all thoughts and ideas would have been erased from the memory but that thread will still be there embedded within the subconscious mind. From then on, the growth of that person will develop and the personality will become more alive, bringing along free will of choice, which is there within every living soul; it's how a person can attune to all the adjustments that there are within their thoughts and subconsciousness.*

*Imagine you have placed in front of you a very long pathway, one that is so long and clear that you can see right to the end without any interruptions or interference; now you place your feet upon the path then suddenly the clarity has gone and there are obstacles in the way. To you the reader, it would become confusing; that is because you are on your own path and have formed an identity for yourself and have learnt how to either choose your own free will of choice or imitate or copy others. To the newborn spirits, it is like an artist with a blank canvas, the clarity of choices is there. It's how they are used which determines how the tapestry of life is formed. Whether the choices are good or bad it is how they are dealt with which determines how your life will transpire.*

*As a person grows and develops into adulthood, their life would be faced with many challenges, to some people they would be able to manoeuvre themselves around these challenges and adapt to certain changes easily, allowing themselves to continue to walk forward and move on. These types of people would embrace and enjoy the challenge and would make the most of every atom of time they have to explore the new pathway, they would easily accept each change as a gift of knowledge that is placed in front of them.*

*To others, changes in their life can be unsettling, challenging and sometimes disturbing. Life suddenly becomes unclear as to how to adjust to the new changes that are arising. We would encourage people to accept the new challenges that they are being faced with as a new pathway for them to explore and enjoy. We understand that at times a certain amount of courage and strength is required to be able to accept the changes that are there, in some cases it's likened to stepping into a new life, old familiar faces and places are still there but it is like that blank canvas has come back to life for you to start all over again.*

*When a much-loved one is lost back to Spirit the person left behind upon the earth has massive changes to their life as well as adjusting to the loss and living without that person. Grief is like an unseen shadow that envelopes around a person, consuming them within its power; it is personal to all and a difficult path to walk upon. To the newly returned Spirit, they quickly adjust to be able to direct as much love as they can to their loved ones back upon the earth; their presence may not always be felt but their love will be directed to those left behind.*

*To accept this kind of change is challenging but with time the grief becomes like a comfortable overcoat of acceptance where the wearer will be able to move on but will always have those precious memories to help guide them through the rest of their life. Changes can happen at any time in a person's life, whether invited or not, accept and embrace the change as a challenge that you will be able to conquer.*

*24 March 2023*

*Grey Dove, Black Feathers and Josiah*

All our learning is direct from Spirit. These meeting notes will give you an idea of the instruction we receive to weave within these pages. Nothing is fabricated or taken from other sources. Each spiritual relationship is different in the same way as characters and personalities we already know from our earthly group of friends. This meeting lasted for over an hour. Janet only paused for a glass of water. The energies come and go once they made their point. Just like any normal conversation.

Grey Dove:

*So, my friend, I'm going to continue now that the meeting is open and your aura has expanded so we can continue with the task in hand, which is, as always, that we can use her energies, her mind and her vocal cords so we can transmit our words. Many people will think how clever this is done. It is nothing marvellous. It is something we can do with certain people on the earth. It is to do with the energies. Everyone has an aura. It is your energy field. It is very personal to you. It is like the invisible you that is with you all the time. It is like an overcoat that stretches inwards and outwards around your body. It is the energy that is your soul, your Spirit, although that is deep within you. Imagine where your solar plexus is where your emotions are.*

*It emanates like an energy field that surrounds you. It is individual to everyone. When we choose our Mediums or people who we are working with is often done when you are back in Spirit. It is linked to how much that spiritual knowledge is within a particular energy when they are in the realms. They choose that when they come back, they are going to become a vessel to be used by the spiritual energies. When that person is born, the energies back within the spiritual realms leave people until the time is right. This is unbeknown to them that our energies are blending with their auras. When we feel the time is right, and when we think that person is ready, we let ourselves be known. There is an awful lot of work on our part to blend with their energies so we can work together, the blending of the physical person and our spiritual energies.*

*We start to blend our energies in with Spirit when we are doing this type of work. When we work in trance or channelling Mediumship we go deeper and deeper within the auric field. We can judge the most suitable level to work with. As far as the spiritual energies are concerned, everyone is equal, from someone giving healing by holding someone's hand. No one is higher or lower. You are on the same equal footing. There are many ways that you can work with Spirit with the first levels of healing and clairvoyance before going deeper.*

*It's very hard for people to envision another world. If you try to speak about another country that is known to you, it comes straight into your mind and you can imagine the people and buildings within it. But if someone was to mention a country you have never heard of, you will find it very hard to envision what that country is like.*

*Take that thought further. How would you describe the spiritual world, about another planet, another world? The surprise is this. We are in the ether and all around you, here, now, on this planet. This is where the energy is coming from, and it is also in the mind of the Medium who is working alongside the energy from inside the atmosphere. Our world is created within your imagination.*

*When we are working with her, we can create a great orb of energy around her. Her light is bright and buzzing. Not everyone works like that, everyone is different. There are many who work on a deeper vibration than her. Some go so deep that the energy they are talking to can change their voice vibration to become the voice of that energy. We work with everyone differently depending on how that person would cope.*

Black Feathers:

*I would never dare to challenge any of the words of Grey Dove or any of the other energies. I wanted to leap in to add my point about the energies. It's like atoms of energy that are around each and every one of you. It is a shame really that you can't look outside your body to see what is happening in the atmosphere. When you are in your physical body, you can't see everything very clearly. It would be a fascinating thought, my friend, if you could step out and see how it actually is. You only get that privilege when you come back to Spirit.*

Running Water:

*We are becoming deeper due to the way we are working. There is an energy who wants to come and say hello to you.*

Josiah:

*My dear friend, it is Josiah. I praise the dear Lord for allowing my energies to come through. I've been in my room with tired eyes. Take it within your heart to thank the Lord every evening for the breath within your body and for everyone who are dear to you. Life is like a stepping stone. Every day when you wake up you step on another stone, another rung of the ladder, you are walking forward all the time, you don't go backwards. Time is moving on. Time is like that soldier who is at the front with a banner marching forward. He can pave the way forward. It is that invisible cloak that is there. Take it within your heart to thank the Lord, to thank the heavens, and the spirits who are helping you move forward. I would have my children, my Ruth and my Ezra. You must understand the way I feel because I have not spoken to you for some time. Eliza would say, 'Come, Josiah, time to rest. Take a break, fill your mind of what is happening now and not will become. Everything will start to flow again.' You just need to open that tiny channel in your mind for the energy to flow down. Open up that channel wider. Be patient. Otherwise, your mind will be blocked up. The light will start to shine a lot brighter. That blockage that will be transformed.*

*The closing prayer:*

*From myself, Josiah, I speak on behalf of the Lord, from the Creator, the giver of all. We fill your aura and your light with love and energy. May peace go with you, and you find it within your heart to forgive anyone who has done something unto you that they should not have done. Pass on that forgiveness to everyone who walks within your pathway. Sometimes people concentrate too much on unforgiveness around them and forget to unlock that pathway of forgiveness around them. It may not make it a better world but it will make you a better person.*

*From Josiah, I give you courage, wisdom, peace, happiness and love.*

*Amen.*

*3 July 2023*

*Michael's Fifteenth Session*

It's time for some introductions:

Gilly has been out of circulation for a little while, looking after her mum, who has been a bit poorly. She joined us and picked up where she left off as if she'd never been away interacting with her guides.

Michael has embraced channelling with gusto. He is getting more confident with every session. His guides reflect his joy and vigour of life. No one sleeps while they take the floor with their vibrant, noisy energies.

This was a spectacular evening. It has been chosen to show the depth of feeling, the emotions and solid bond of love between us all, between Heaven and Earth.

Emmanuel was the first to speak through Janet. It was an evening we would not forget. A night of learning, sadness and humour. They tell their stories.

Emmanuel:

*We would like to cover your meeting with protection from the Holy Spirit, love and light. Good evening from Emmanuel. We want to pass on to you and share with everyone on the earth plane so they understand and read our words. At this point, Gilly, we want to welcome you back. It's been a while to let you relax and let the light cascade around you. There is much knowledge to come from your mouth from the words of Spirit. And for Michael, you, too, are being prepared.*

*We are working alongside the spiritual energies on the earth. We are not special. We are just energies here that we have the privilege to work alongside people in this way. You allow us to open up your light. We do not badger or bully you. Contrary to what people say, this is us working together to learn how to blend our energies.*

*Michael, you need to practise when you are on your own*

*so that your energies can get to know you better. It is that development, that advancement, that you have to learn for yourself. Sit and blend those energies in. The more we can blend the more we can get deeper into your consciousness.*

*I come to you, Gilly. You have had a rest but your energies have not rested. They have been helping and guiding you on the journey you had to take in your material life. Before the meeting, conversations were taking place about your mother, and we can tell you that she has been placed in a safe environment with people who care about those with the ailment she has. You can start to let your light shine so the energies can come through. You also need to go back on the path of teaching other people.*

*They also miss the work that you have been doing with them.*

Noah:

*Good evening, Stephen. Ah! My friend, do I give you a name or do you pluck it out of the air? This is Noah. You may have already recognised me. I would like to say that each of you has different kinds of worries. You have stress and anxieties. I want to start with Michael. These are messages so that you can feel better within yourselves. We enjoy this kind of work. If our vessels are feeling down, we want to keep them bright and shiny. Michael, my dear friend, you have found that things are not going the way you'd like. Sometimes plans go astray. I want you to know that you are turning that corner and that things will start to come your way. Tread the boards of somewhere where your services will be very much appreciated.*

*Gilly, everything around you now will start to knit together. The light all around you has been tinged with blue and green, the healing colours. This has been tinged with a brown outer edge that meant that your auric field was quite damaged as you were disturbed with everything that has been going on. All those colours are now blending in together and becoming lighter and lighter. Your mother is being looked after by the angels. You can be rest assured that she is under the best care. She will start to calm down and her quality of life will improve and you will be able to walk along your spiritual pathway. We have brought you back so you can enjoy what you love.*

*Stephen, we give you the energies. We know he has had many messages from us. We also know he has taken a break for a while for our benefit, so he can write up everything and we are pleased with the way you have done this. As we have said, what is the point after weeks of giving knowledge if no one is going to read them? Everything that Spirit does we want it to be shared. To share all that love and light to be shared around the world. We give you heartfelt thanks, my friend, to write up all these words. Once you catch up and have had your break, you will both be able to get together so we can come forth with more words of wisdom. They are words of wisdom and enlightenment.*

*Michael, there are many energies around you, my dear friend. When Michael has finished, Gilly, one of your guides is standing there. He is very impatient but will wait until Michael has finished.*

Michael's guide, the expansive Jimmy, leaps into the conversation to greet Gilly:

*Hello, I'm here again. You're new! How are you? I've never seen you before. It's nice to finally meet you. I've heard your name before. I've been here with these two. They are kind of crazy. I'm high energy. I'm here to start the meeting off and to be very happy. And to make sure everyone has a very good time. My aim is to have fun and be part of this group.*

*But before I go, I want to say hello, and I will see you again soon.*

One of Gilly's guides speaks, a nun from a strict convent from years ago:

*I bring quietness. I bring joy, but peacefully. That's where I came from, an order, a very strict order. We were taught so much about Jesus, the Bible, and like Jimmy, we were often tortured for having the wrong beliefs. Our hands were tied together in prayer. We spent hours studying the Bible and philosophies. We were taught strictness, to toe the line, and not to have our own thoughts. Many had chosen a vow of silence, but I didn't.*

*When I came here* (into Spirit), *I was so ready for torture of the mind. I was so ready for more training and to be bound in Hell for years for thinking differently about our Saviour. We were secretly questioning as that is what an intelligent mind does. An intelligent mind listens and weighs up what it has been told and works out its own truth. We were punished for that, you'll see. Not many of us lived to a very old age. Some of us simply slipped away when possible. We never understood the true order because it was so different to those of people above us – or perceived to be above us. There was cruelty, starvation and death. Deep inside of all of us, we suffered these traumas, sometimes on a day-to-day basis.*

*And yet, we still had this light, this love, this small burning candle of truth. When we came here, it is nothing like what we've been taught. We travelled through universes. We didn't stay in the light, we travelled through it, above and beyond. I spent many years looking out from a small window into the future. I could see mountains, and yet I knew there was something even further than that, over the horizon. I knew there was something, something different.*

*I knew that when this cruelty happened to me, with my hands tied together, in prayer my mind reached out. I didn't know where it went. But now I do. It came to the upper echelons. I stretched my mind through the cruelty of the physical level it came up high. I realise it was me that was the teacher. I taught forbearance. I dried many tears. I was the teacher but I never knew. I realise that between here and eternity there are millions of souls all waiting to have their tears dried and that on this level, we can do that. But on your level, it is difficult.*

*There are passings of many souls, tortured in their minds. We must learn to realise that our imaginations, our flights of fancy, are our truth of love and light. There are many beings who will speak this evening, but there is one who will come to talk. Listen to his kind words. They are way above religion, the Bible. There is a truth, a light that none can describe. That is what I teach. Thank you.*

Mary:

*There have been many wise words that have been uttered by them. This is Mary, Stephen. First of all, I would like to place a blessing over every one of your heads. I would like to speak about the energies that are channelling through this evening when they speak of torture and physical attack and abuse when they were on the earth. It's hard to believe that these attacks are still being carried out in these modern times. There is much cruelty going on the earth behind closed and locked doors. And yes, some of them are going on in orders of religious beliefs.*

*When we were on the earth, we found that whatever the belief in your soul, within your heart, it is every person's choice of which religious belief that people feel deep within them. Sometimes people follow religions because they've been born into it. They've been brought up and told this is where you go to church or synagogue of temples where these religions are taking place. We have spoken about this many times before. It is not until you get older when you start to understand what you've been listening to. Sometimes there is manipulation in these religious groups.*

*Spirits have been around forever. Spirits have been in the atmosphere, the ether, for an eternity. A few years back, spirituality was classed as a religion. So, it's put into the category of religious beliefs. Where people follow what they believe in. At times, people from other beliefs and religious groups, we are recognised as a religion. There is a God, the Creator, God is the giver of life. People who are outside our beliefs say that once you are dead – that is the end of that. Your soul goes off somewhere and is never allowed to make contact or be recovered again. That is because their minds are closed to the fact of the universal belief of existence. Yes, we are all in the universe, the ether and it is energy.*

*Many religious beliefs deny that because they say it is their religion is the one that you should follow. Sometimes these religions torture and blackmail people to be made to feel guilty. They say that you are a sinner if you do anything wrong. Ever since man has walked upon the earth, they've always done wrong. That is the way that people learn to do right because they have done wrong. This is learning from your mistakes. To maim someone intentionally to force them into believing what you want them to believe, that is wrong. That is a criminal sin, my friend.*

*You know me as Mary. You know my energies as when I was on the earth. I am the influence of that person who would have born the person who made greatness on this earth. Now that I am back in Spirit, we recognise that we are Spirit and that the beliefs I had when I was back on the earth are still there. We are not more open-minded in Spirit because many of the religions and beliefs are man-made. They are what someone who felt they had a calling. These may go back thousands of years. After a calling, they get a gathering who may be weak in mind or they start to get a belief and it goes wider and wider. Then all the offshoot groups form over thousands of years. People always need something to believe in, to follow. It's like handing your life over to something to believe in.*

*I was listening to the story from Michael from the very lively energy (about being tortured). He harbours no ill feeling now he is in Spirit. He is a very lively character. It is not a mask; it is just happiness now that he is back in Spirit. He realises that when he was back on earth, his fate was in the hands of other people. His energy, they could not strip his personality. Now he is back in Spirit he is a very lively person.*

*We also listened with much interest – I say 'we', my friend, because there are many of us here. We know who is going to come through as we encourage certain energies to come through and give their stories so that people on the earth can hear the stories of energies who led a life on earth. I am going to step back so that someone else can come through and say a few words.*

It's Christina:

*Good evening, Steve, it's Christina. I just wanted to say to Gilly that I'm so sorry for the energy that came through speaking about their past life and their existence. It sounds like something that many people would not want to put their ears to. When I was a young teenager, it was decided that I would go into the convent. I can say from my heart that I had a lovely experience there. There was strictness where we were but I can say that love would touch me every living moment of that day.*

*To hear and listen to stories where people were cajoled into what they were forced to do with their hands being tied. It was quite alien to me. We do know these things happen in your world. Here, in Spirit, we do encourage other energies to come through and tell their stories. It is happening now, being locked behind doors and being badly treated because someone who thinks they are better than them wants to make people suffer. Their minds can get distorted. When they come back to Spirit, these people who've done harm need to see what damage they have done to others before they can progress. They need to cover themselves in forgiveness to cleanse themselves. They need to stay in the realms until they can go back into another incarnation.*

*Michael, you have a visitor. We speak to Jimmy, and we know he makes Janet jump very high off her chair when he comes through. Before we let this energy come through, we want to say welcome, Gilly. It is a wonderful moment when we knew you were going to come along. I want to cover you in the light of love. I want to say a very quick prayer. I'm not going to close the meeting. I just want to say:*

*Dear God, I want you to keep Gilly safe and cover her in all the light that the angels can spin all around her so her mind can go back into more normality and that her mother is kept safe as houses and that all the angels on the earth and in Spirit are looking after her. Amen.*

*Michael, as Charlie would say, you can open up the hatch and let your energy through.*

Michael's new energy:

*Good evening, everybody. It is a pleasure to see you all again. I say hello, young lady. It is a pleasure to be amongst friends, visible and invisible. I come from a realm from above the sky. They are so bright you cannot imagine. It is in that space where we learn and grow as spirits and other spirits learn and grow. You are part of that circle of Spirit, that circle of life that never ends. The everlasting endless life. It's a life you must treasure and a light that you must go to. It is the light that helps you on the earth plane and the light that you must seek to find things on this earth plane. It is the light that convinces you that we exist. And for you to learn how you can communicate with people on your earth plane. You see we who are up here and around you to support you. Our task is for us in the invisible world to get to know as many on your world as can be.*

*There are many who do not believe in the existence of the invisible world. It is the discovery of us for those people. In the end, they all go back to Spirit, as we all know. It is an incredibly important time at the moment.*

*The world is going through such a big shake, a much-needed shake. Vibrations are rising at an extremely fast rate. There will be casualties, but there are others who will be rising above this. Ultimately, people need to shift and become part of the cause and part of the effect of what will happen to the earth. I want you all to know you will never be left to be undecided what to do when it comes to your spirituality and your connection to us. You will never be left alone to understand who and what you connect to. The spirits above the sky are teaching me, are teaching you, and are teaching him and her. They are the ones who gather in this circle to help the other energies to come through. They are connected to the individual. I want you to remember that. Be with Spirit at all times as the Spirit will be with you. I will say goodbye.*

Running Water:

*We welcome you, Gilly. We understand the traumas you've been going through. We understand your devotion had to go to your mother as she needed your help. Her mind is deeply disturbed. It is the ageing process.*

*I would like to say to Michael that you have many energies that have been attracted to our group. They have asked permission over the coming months to be able to come and join within your own energy. We are going to pre-warn you that you will have many invisible friends. Some of them will stay and some of them will not. It is like the blending of energies with Janet and Gilly over the years. You will get energies who will attach themselves to your aura. It is like when you join a circle. At first it may feel right, but then you will want to join another. The energies go from one person to another. You will be having some more interesting energies that will come through. We need to keep the protection all around you.*

*It's time to close the meeting in prayer:*

*May the heavens above your heads continue to guide you in the right direction. Continue to teach you right from wrong and to do unto others what you want to be done to yourself. Always be courteous and polite. Throw being judgemental out of the window. Take people for how they are. Not what you see on the surface but it is the inner part of the person we see. We see their emotions, their lights that ebb and flow backwards and forwards that's nestled deep within yourself. We ask you to open your minds. You are all Spirit within the human body. Try to see that light for yourself rather than the package that's on the outside where people will pass judgement.*

*Spread love and forgiveness around the world. If you can combine the two together it comes into the great ball of positivity that drives negativity away. Negativity grows and grows. Positivity may be smaller but it is stronger. And it will always exhaust that negative energy.*

*From the spiritual realms, from the Creator, we give you love, we give you peace. Amen.*

We're about to close this chapter and open the next. In reading these conversations there's one very human trait that comes across. Our guides get pleasure and excited about their words being spoken and listened to on Earth. The act of channelling and making a connection is as satisfying and enjoyable for us both. It is heartwarming. In Part Two, Chapter Eleven, we will explore spirituality with an infinite, universal dimension.

# Blog

*How Can You Explain the Unexplainable?*

*Science or Spirituality or Both?*

This is a tricky one. In your heart, if you believe in Spirit, how can you support your argument to someone who trashes the idea, saying it's all nonsense? That science has all the answers, that biology, physiology, psychology, neurology, and all the other 'ologies' dismiss your flimsy emotional argument as make-believe? Then to pile insult upon injury to say: 'Isn't it about time you lived in the real world?'

Where do you start? You can't challenge the achievements of science and medicine of mankind's ability to learn and develop over the centuries and even create vaccines for killer viruses.

I guess this is where you search for connections. Of understanding intelligence, of the workings of the brain, that's a good place to start, but that can only get you so far. At some point your thought processes bang up against the invisible energies that surround us. Energies that surf our minds and bodies in electric waves. Energies that stimulate thought and trigger inspiration. Energies that reveal themselves in grit and determination, in resilience, in hope, of expectation. Of the greatest mystery of all, love. Certainly, we can fit heart and blood-pressure monitors to measure on bleeping graphs the effect of falling in love. But where does that spark come from? Yes, science can describe and measure it. Science can analyse it. At the end of the tests, how do they explain the magic? That's one formula beyond their reach.

This is the connection, the crossover point, where the mystery of life is the combination of science and Spirit. This is living in the real world, a wondrous world of the known and unknown, a world of blissful expectation.

Perhaps it is only when we graduate from this world into the next that we will reach a true level of knowledge and understanding. The next world is one that should hold no fear. These are the words of Morning Mist, a Spirit Guide:

'There is no darkness when a person's life ends. There is light and love and pure happiness.'

In the end, you realise that science and Spirit are one and the same creative force. One is driven by the other.

## Coming Next

*Healing Energy – The Force Within*

Grey Dove touched on what the world of Spirit looks like when he mentioned the Halls of Learning. We will come to that in the second part of the book. Before then, Chapter Six will focus on healing in general and spiritual healing in particular.

Positive energy is the fulfilling power of Spirit. It drives the emotional, mental and physical us, the Mind, Body and Spirit, if you will. It fuels spiritual healing. Healing is dedicated to one of the most important elements in the heavenly toolbox. It is another skill channelled and directed by those acting as a beneficial link with Spirit. Caring souls are acting as a Medium even if they aren't aware of the role they've just played. They are working with Spirit out of love.

# Six

# Healing Energy

*The Force Within*

You have ears to listen
You have a voice to soothe
You have hands to touch
You have care to give

To sit and listen. To wait patiently. To be there for someone without a ticking clock. To witness sadness, worry, doubt, fear or any guilt flow from anxious tears. A soothing voice, a gentle touch of the hand. These are sublime expressions of loving care. These are the subtle, silent waves of healing.

They are the invisible but powerful energies. Active energies are channelled through mind and thought. Energy healing complements the body's ability to heal itself and be in concert with accepted medical practice. Energy healing alone cannot claim to cure disease or broken bones or address mental health issues or other medical complaints. It can and does help recovery and restore calm and tranquillity to include alleviating stress, anxiety, pain, depression, insomnia, trauma and grief.

It is the same divine energy that channels through the minds and thoughts of Mediums and healers treat their patients. The starting point is the same. They set their intention to direct the energy with the purpose of healing. They prepare themselves by being in the right frame of mind. They put their own outside pressures to one side. When working with Spirit, they connect with their guides. It is a great help to bring affirmations like these to mind before they begin to transfer energy.

- I am a channel of love, light and care.
- I am the pathway of divine healing energy for mind and body.
- I will be attuned with my healing guides to direct their spiritual guidance.
- I have confidence and trust in my healing intuition.
- I welcome the healing energies flowing through the palms of my hands and mind.

Janet has been trained under the guidelines of the Spiritualists National Union (SNU). The SNU defines spiritual healing as 'a form of healing by the use of forces and energies from the world of Spirit channelled through healing Mediums'. Janet has been practising for many years and is now the lead healer in her local spiritual church. My mode of healing is Reiki. Becoming a Reiki Master is my next step with the Reiki Academy of London. There are Codes of Conduct and legal guidelines that must be observed when providing energy healing.

We have to be respectful as the subject of energy healing, either spiritually or via Reiki, deserve books in their own right. With this in mind, we will provide a topline introduction that may inspire you to learn more. To this end, you'll find contact details in the reference section in Appendix Two.

This note from the SNU introduction makes the interesting point that energy healing is not linked with a person's religious beliefs or any belief at all:

'There is a tendency for people to think that spiritual healing is effective only owing to the faith or belief of the person requesting this form of treatment.'

This is not true.

Spiritual healing requires no faith or belief whatsoever on the part of the person seeking healing. Nor is it necessary for a person to have the same belief as that of the healing Medium administering the healing.

The actual healing itself is one of a spiritual nature and this has an effect on all levels: mentally, emotionally, physically and spiritually. Would you like to imagine receiving some Reiki?

You'd be lying on your back on a bed or couch. This is to allow a Reiki healer to move around from head to toe.

They'll make you feel comfortable. A pillow is placed under your head and maybe another under your knees. As your body can cool during a session, a soft lightweight blanket will cover you. Bare feet or socks. No shoes or trainers. A glass of water for a sip before and after is to hand. Some soothing, gentle music is playing, a Reiki recording with five-minute excerpts helps pace the treatment. The healing session will last for half an hour or more. The idea is to create a relaxing atmosphere with dimmed lights and sweet fragrances to help you focus on yourself and let the world outside recede into unimportance.

Relax and close your eyes. You may even fall asleep. You'll be asked if you have any physical pains or if you're feeling stressed or anxious. The healer will ask permission for either placing hands on or off your body. The penetrative healing effect will be the same either way. You will be made aware of the Code of Conduct to avoid any personal or delicate parts of the body being touched. With hands-on, palms simply rest on a particular position, with no extra downward pressure.

The Mikao Usui Japanese Tradition of Reiki commences.

The healer will quietly connect with Reiki energies. They'll stand in silence to cleanse their aura with a motion of hands across their arms, sweeping left and right. This is a symbolic dry-brushing of their aura to signal to the Reiki gods as they prepare to receive and transfer Reiki energy to you.

The healer will place hands together in a prayer-like stance by their heart chakra. This signals the intention to begin giving Reiki. This position is called Gassho.

Their hands will be placed in one of twelve positions around your head and body, moving slowly to your toes. As this happens, healing palms will begin to channel and direct energy. You will feel a warming or cooling sensation depending on the nature of need. For example, an inflamed knee may need cooling, a strained muscle may need gentle warming.

The healer can feel an electric tingling in their palms. This pulsing can spike and become exaggerated if Reiki senses points of pain or stress needing attention.

If you're living a fast-track stressful life, healing may be centred on your head. If you're in an emotional maelstrom then heart and solar plexus chakras may be crying out for attention. When the session is over, this may be signalled by a light squeeze of the shoulder. Afterwards, you can stay within a peaceful state of repose before waking. The session would end with the practitioner smoothing down your aura along your body and adopting the Gassho stance again to thank Reiki for the gift of healing.

Practitioners are always developing their skills and sensitivities. They can learn to enhance their ability by sharpening their levels of intuition using symbols relating to Earth, Heaven, and Distance Healing. The distance or oneness symbol crosses time and space. This involves sending healing energy by mind and thought to help someone anywhere in the world. It's important to know that Reiki practitioners should not attempt to diagnose any mental or physical condition. They are not doctors in the medical sense but healers using spiritual energy.

I trained for the Reiki 1 and 2 Diploma with the Centre of Excellence, as well as the Reiki Academy of London. In the introductory notes these conditions were listed where Reiki treatment could be effective. They included stress, anxiety, insomnia, OCD, depression, pain, hormonal imbalances, toxic symptoms, fatigue, grief and trauma.

Here is a real-life example requested on a UK Facebook post:

*Hello Reiki community, please can you send healing to my cousin who has suddenly been admitted to hospital with a brain tumour. Location: Langley Hospital, British Columbia, Canada. Thank you.*

To go deeper and learn more about Reiki, please refer to the link on the source information page in Appendix Two.

Emmanuel wanted to say more about illness and healing:

*3 October 2022*

*Michael's Training Session*

*Good evening, my friends, this is Emmanuel. When we bring our energies through, we do not prepare what we are going to say. We do not scribble words on parchment. We are all friends. We do not prepare speeches before the meeting. Conversations take place when topics pop into our minds. What I wanted to speak about today is your well-being.*

*You are all individuals in our own right. You will be able to cope with illnesses and link in with the spiritual energies to get healing alongside any healing you will be getting from your doctors. Your well-being is not only about your physical bodies, it is your mental state as well that you have within you. If you take away your body, you have your soul, your Spirit.*

*In Spirit, there are no illnesses. In Spirit, everything is purified. There are no illnesses here. Your thoughts are clear. In your physical well-being, you have both your body and soul together on the earth. You need to look after both. People look after their bodies, they run, they keep fit, they do many exercises. This is all good for the brain, the mind as well. It is the mental part of your physical being that's connected with your soul, your Spirit. It is your Spirit that you need to be kind to. People often think, 'What's the difference?' They think that the body and Spirit come together as one. They're not. They separate at death, when the body is no longer of use. You need to treat them separately because they are your emotional toolbox. You need to give it love. You need to love yourself. Unless you can love yourself, how can you give love to others? This is something you should think about. There is so much that goes on in people's minds. What you practise, what you say during the day, it's like you switch to automatic mode. You speak, you do actions, but you do not put a lot of thought into what you are actually doing with your Spirit.*

*You could mentally visualise yourself laying your body down and looking at your soul. How would you like to see it? Shining brightly? Sparkling with a happy hue all around it? Or, would you want to see your soul just lying there, deadpan? If you put that back in your body, how would you react?*

*If you visualise your soul shining bright, you would feel happy and light-hearted. If you lay your soul down and envision it as a dowdy colour or hue, it would bring you down. There is a phrase on the earth, 'Take a good look at yourself'. Look in the mirror and what do you see? Don't take your soul for granted. It is your personality. Your Spirit is the essence of you. Your body has to be nurtured and looked after as it is the vessel that's keeping you on the earth. Put the two together, they become one, but both need to be treated with love and respect separately. Does this make sense? Sometimes people would not understand what we are saying. We try not to go too deep. People like light-hearted messages. We do not want to get bogged down with philosophy. We want things to be done with simplicity and clarity, with clear vision and clear hearing so that people can instantly connect with what they are reading. I hope this makes sense.*

*I will now withdraw my energies.*

## *Healing from the Heart of Christina*

You've met Sister Theresa with her birth name Christina, in the previous chapter. She is the most loving and caring Spirit. When she was fifteen, she entered the convent and spent most of her time in the hospital ward. She died in her mid-thirties of an infection caught from one of her patients.

Over the months she has spoken about the most sensitive aspects of spiritual healing: mental, physical and emotional. She has spoken about people who have taken their own lives and about parents who've lost a child.

We give you her words:

*It's such a joy to be able to come and converse. The reason I wanted to say this is that the souls that have come over, and there are many of them, I want to concentrate on the ones that are coming from war-torn countries, or those from sudden deaths or people who have taken their own lives we give them the healing they need. Their souls need comfort to adjust to the spiritual world.*

*When a life is taken very quickly, sometimes it takes that energy quite a while to understand that they have actually passed. They instantly become happy because their soul knows they have passed from their physical being. They know they have been taken quickly and roughly from the earth plane. That's what we have been doing. I have been with many of the children.*

*For every parent that has lost a child, it is important for them to know that their child is always being looked after by the angels and by the Sisters of Mercy. We don't have to heal their souls in the sense we have to do with an adult because they have been on earth for such a short time that they would not have had many interruptions to affect that soul.*

Little children and their parents, Christina continues:

*I've been looking after all the little children within the spiritual realms that have been coming back from your world. They come into this place; I like to call it our little paradise because it is really like a little paradise for these energies that have come over.*

*It does not stop there because just think that when a child dies, or anyone dies, they go into the Resting Period. No, my friend, our main work is with the parents that have been left behind, because they are the bereft. They are the ones that are grieving. They are the ones that have this pain, this physical pain you cannot see, you cannot touch. Nothing can cure it because their offspring have been taken. There is a whole band of us. That's where we concentrate all our thoughts and love into these people.*

*If you had been speaking to someone who had just lost their small child, I cannot imagine how you would cope. I'll tell you how you would cope: all the angels, all the energies like us would band around for that strength, that courage within your aura to have the strength to keep walking forward and forward. And as each day goes by without my dear darling child, we need to continue pouring that strength and energy down to parents so they can keep putting one foot forward. It is very interesting over here; I know we have met. I wanted to say that I am a sister, a nurse, a carer, a healer, within the Halls of Caring, it's not all children that come to us but the majority are, as that's the path I chose.*

She adds:

*You know I am in the ward of the children who've come over. We want every mother, father and guardian to know that when the children come over, they are very joyous in the spiritual realms as we heal their little souls. I find this very addictive, and I let my words flow. Sister Immaculata says, Christina, you should really take a vow of silence, but that would be like purgatory to me.*

Caring for returning souls who were not like anyone else.

*I'm going to speak about the patients in the infirmary where I've been working. I'm not speaking about when I was on the earth. I'm speaking about now. It's the children that we look after who come over from traumatic passings, and some who when they were on the earth their minds may not have been made exactly how people thought their minds should be. Their minds would be impaired and maybe their physical bodies as well. And sometimes they may have not made sense of their lives but their light would have been flickering away inside them. If someone is different from the way they should be, people say they are abnormal, that they have mental or physical dysfunction. When these energies come back to Spirit, we have many of them, we heal their souls and take them out of the infirmary so they can start their spiritual journey again.*

### *The Pain of Suicide*

Spirit has a compassionate attitude to those who have taken their own lives. They may have been under extreme mental or emotional stress. Sometimes in this modern world it is understandable for some to become totally overwhelmed with pressure and lose all hope. Their self-chosen exit was part of their long-term incarnation pathway to return to Spirit. Their spiritual progression continues as a learning experience in their book of life.

Running Water gave permission for this message to me:

*There is an energy here, it is a gentleman. He wants to come, and we have given permission. Sometimes we like to allow these things to show how delicate the energies are.*

*This gentleman would have been a friend of yours. He says he ended his life because he felt he had no more life left in him to continue upon the earth. He says he's sorry and asks forgiveness.*

That message was from my best friend, who I was at school with in Singapore at the RAF Changi Grammar School. It was his action and the subsequent message of proof twenty-three years ago from a Medium that began my role as a writer for Spirit.

### *Grief is a Testament to Love*

There's a common phrase, 'Grief is the price you pay for love'. Be it for a friend, loved one or family pet. Recently, I was asked to become the celebrant at my beloved uncle's funeral. He was so full of life. A real one-off who broke the accepted rules of a serving RAF Officer by being slightly disrespectful of authority. Everyone loved him. He drank deeply from the pleasures of living.

We all had our special memories. Accessing them made us laugh. He was a lovable rogue, always a twinkle in his eye. He transmitted joy. I merely said that whenever you're feeling melancholy, simply run that private video in your head and any blue clouds will disappear.

That's my grief medicine for you. Think about not what you've lost but what you gained from knowing that special someone. Think about the love and the help they gave to make you who you are. Today, this minute. Wear your grief as a badge of honour. Surge forward to achieve all that life has to offer in their memory. Remember, they are always with you.

Their Spirit loving your Spirit. Their angel is on your shoulder, a constant companion. Use sadness as the spur to happiness. Don't let grief paralyse you. Respect it, live with it, and move on in praise of them. That's what they would want.

It feels right for Christina to say a closing prayer for this chapter:

*From the Divine, from the heart of Jesus and from all the energies that are over here, I just like to give thanks to all the spiritual energies who give up their time to come and work with all the people on the earth, and I'd like to give thanks to all the Mediums who give up their time to be able to connect with the spiritual energies to brush their auras and come through to give out words of wisdom. I want to send out love to all the people on the earth who are suffering with their mental ability. We do not forget people who have been hurt by words that have been said carelessly from people's mouths. I want to say:*

*From the dear Lord, the Creator, and from dear Mary that the earth is being clothed in a blanket of gold and blue that is for love and protection. May the good Lord go with you. Amen.*

## Blog

*Angels Are Around Us*

You know you have a guardian angel. One that's around you, supporting you, loving and protecting you. This note is from

Josiah, a wise spiritual guide. If you thought there was only one kind of angel, think again. These are his words:

There are earth angels, Spirit angels and heavenly angels.

> The Earth Angel. *Is someone who is there at the precise moment in time when they are needed, whether it be to help a person by listening to them, by comforting them in sad times, to aid them by helping them to cross the road to see them safely on the other side. There are many of them on the earth, they have no labels, they are just full of goodness within themselves to help those in need, they have been given a mission by the Spirit guardians to help many on the earth.*
>
> The Spirit Angels. *These are the energies who are there ready and waiting when the returned soul transcends through the light back to the Homeland, they have many labels: Sisters of Mercy, carers, nurses and doctors, any energy who is willing to help to comfort the returning soul to give them reassurance that now their earth time is over they are back in the Homeland surrounded by love and peace.*
>
> Heavenly Angels. *The description of these angelic spirits is of the purest light that has never been part of the physical world; their mission is to welcome back the newborn or any energy that has not been affected by the physical world. These angels have been untouched by human intervention.*

Here's a poem by Josiah.

**Angel of the Night**

The colour of the sky is ink black
Yet the air is crystal clear
There is a shadow across the moon
Did you see it move? Where did it go?
It is unseen against the blackness of the sky
Yet you can see the wings flutter in the darkness
You can feel the love float in from the breeze.

There it is again, up against the light of the moon
Ahh, it is the Angel of the Night keeping watch
It looks, it sees, it blinks its eyes
It flutters its wings then the stars shine like twinkling lights
And showers the world with love and protection
You are never alone when the Angel of the Night is there
She is the mother of all for your protection
When the dawn breaks, she rests her wings until dusk
Then her nightly vigil will once again take place.

Keep safe, my children of the earth
Your lives are precious gifts
You were sent from us to live a life
Cherish your days on the earth
Love your brothers and sisters
You are all God's children.

Shake your neighbour's hand with a smile upon your face
Forgo wars and hatred instead unite and love
You all live as one under God's sky

Breathe in the warmth and the love which He sends to you
For you all are the children of God.

My energies will now retire, your forever friend Josiah.

## Coming Next

*As One with Nature*

We are as one with planet earth. We are spiritual beings co-existing and dependent upon all the other elements of creation. The ground we walk upon, the air we breathe, the trees and plants that sustain us, the animals and birds are temporary earthbound spirits. The same as we are.

In short, we need to be in harmony with nature. Where would we be without bees?

# Seven

## As One with Nature

These quotes are from representatives of First Nation Indigenous Civilisations. They've been taken from the World Economic Forum meeting January 13 2022.

Don Sebastian of the Inca People in Peru:

> *'We have to restore our harmony with Mother Earth in order to enjoy a harmonious and full life. If we don't do this, we will continue to live with hatred, jealousy and sickness. But before that, Mother Earth has to forgive us for having hurt her so much.'*

Vandria Borari of the Borari people in Brazil:

*'When Mother Earth gets sick, we get sick. The river, the forest and the animals – they complete our lives, and they are the reason of our existxence.'*

Carlos Barrios of the Mayan people in Guatemala:

*'Mother Earth and human beings have the same purpose – to grow, to go towards an evolutionary moment. The most important thing in this life is your own self. If you take responsibility and you create the development of your own self, you're going to help not just you, you're going to help humanity.'*

We are custodians and agents of positive change. It is your spiritual self that will drive change. Planet Earth is alive from central core to open surface and feels the pain we inflict.

*'Our spirituality is a oneness and an interconnectedness with all that lives and breathes, even with all that does not live or breathe.'*

*Mudrooroo, Aboriginal writer.*

Black Feathers wanted to add his thoughts:

*Many people will be interested in the trees, woodland areas, the grasses because they can feel the Spirit in the trees. When they place their hands on the tree, they can feel the life in that tree. They can feel the energy that is coming up from the earth. It gives people pleasure. They can look out to the oceans all they see is water but that can give them a sense of movement and life under the water. When they look up into the sky, they can see and wonder what goes on in the sky. It is something about the elements you have within you that can make people feel the energy. You can find that energy within you that can unlock that doubt and to place into words. It is all part of the great Spirit that has been given to you. It is something that should not be denied. It is the same with the animals. Everyone has their spiritual animals with you.*

*Within the spiritual realms, you have another realm where the animals are, but in fact, it is all side by side within the ether, very strongly with the Native Americans and in the far-flung places where the animals are very important. Believe and trust in us as we will never let you down. My friend, our frustration ebbs very quickly and now I want to continue on the theme of the animals. It is common knowledge that some of the animals are very precious, where man feels it is their right to kill this animal for properties they may have within them for ornaments, for clothing, for things they can sell. Is disastrous a catastrophe. It still goes on. They are being taken from your earth and some of them will become extinct; man is doing this for their own gain.*

*We are here to make contact to prove that life is indeed continuous. We can't tell man how to run their lives. Everyone has conscience to tell you right from wrong. Some people think it is right to kill for monetary gain. They think that animals do not have feelings or senses. An animal may have more senses than a human. They have their instincts. Animals kill for survival not for fun. Some of them are the most beautiful creatures on the earth.*

*Man lets his conscious go to sleep. Everything on earth is there for a reason. Place some of this within the pages of your book. But people we are talking about are not interested in your book or the spiritual energies at all. They are just interested in what they feel is in their interest. They will find out when they get back then they will feel remorse, they cut down trees and burn grasses and wipe out vegetation. You have to have people who place regulations to stop people doing this.*

Black Feathers talked about animals having feelings. All pet owners and those who work with animals know this to be true. Here's a paragraph about such a bond from a friend and her horse 'Jack' and describes them getting to know each other:

*Jack is a wonderful character and a nice person, but being a prey animal, that inbuilt instinct to be suspicious of just about everything is quite strong in him. He is so expressive. You can read what he is thinking by the look on his face! In the early days he was nervous of having his legs washed, being tied up, having a rug taken off, being clipped, having his mane pulled, putting a fly mask on, traffic, etc. But he never objected in an obnoxious or dangerous way. It was always a very quiet and measured response to something he wasn't sure about.*

*During the first six months we began to get to know each other and work out how we both ticked. I learnt enough about him in those early days to know I wanted to keep him with me. Over the years we have built up a partnership and trust and I have learnt how to handle him and what not to do to worry or stress him out.*

*A small story as an example: My friend and I were taking Jack and Reilly (her horse) on holiday to north Dorset. I always travel Jack in a leather head collar as they say it will break in an accident, whereas a synthetic one won't. I only ever use it for travelling him. We arrived at our destination and as usual turned them out for a couple of hours to get over the journey while we had coffee and cake before going for a ride. Coffee and yummy cake consumed, we went to catch them both, but I had forgotten to bring his everyday head collar, so took the leather one out to the field with me.*

*Jack was like, 'Oh, hi, Mum!' until I was two inches from his nose with the alien leather head collar! He took one sniff of it, decided it wasn't his and I was clearly going to kill him with it and walked off and wouldn't let me catch him. We eventually corralled him and got on with our ride. I phoned ahead to two friends who were joining us from another yard and had to ask them to swing by my yard and pick up 'his head collar' for me to avoid having to chase him around the paddock every day! The yard staff have had to learn this one as well! I often tell people that as long as you know them and play by Jack's rules, everything will be okay!*

She added this note about prey animals and their natures:

*A prey animal is an animal that is hunted or killed by another animal for food. Now I know there isn't a lot of that going on in Wiltshire, but in times gone by, or even in places like Kenya today, where the horses we were recently riding had been hunted by lion, a horse would be considered prey. Horses are highly perceptive of their surroundings and their defence is to flee quickly from danger at a moment's notice; it is an inherent part of their nature.*

For myself, the pangolin is one of my favourite animals. There's an organisation Fauna & Flora that helps to protect this wonderful creature. David Attenborough is their vice president. You'll find their details and those of other organisations concerned with conservation, restoration and renewal at the end of the book.

We know that every living being in the animal world is spiritual. We know they communicate with humans and with each other using a combination of visual, auditory and tactile signals. Telepathy is a fourth.

The first time I experienced this was during a service at the Maidenhead Spiritual Church. Janet had begun her demonstration of Mediumship. As usual she'd waited for Spirit to point her to the person in the congregation to receive the first message. The way she works is for her arm to swing left or right until she identifies spirits contact. Seconds passed. In those seconds, Spirit downloads the description of the Spirit-side messenger to her. A jolt of surprise startles the recipient as they realise they've been singled out from all the other people in the room. 'I have your mother, grandfather, sister, brother, friend or whoever here.' She describes them and passes on the message. The service continues and person by person is singled out.

So far, so normal. Then the extraordinary happened.

Toby, a Tibetan Spaniel, had woken from a lovely sleep on his rug in front of the platform. Toby goes for a stroll. He's happy, quite at home in the church he knows so well. Very comfortable. He's met Janet a number of times. Old friends.

He knows her voice. She's speaking to someone. In mid-sentence Janet pauses and turns to Toby's owner, who's acting as the service host for us.

'Sharon, I've got Toby here. He wants you to know you need to change his diet, he feels bloated. Cut down on those chocolate treats. His left hind leg is itchy too and needs your attention.'

You could've heard a pin drop.

## Blog

*Your Heart Is in Your Head*

Or more specifically, your emotional heart is inside your mind. During this life you are Spirit in an earthly guise, in human form. At birth, you were pure of Spirit. You brought with you hard evidence of your spiritual nature. They provide proof of your spirituality. You feel them but cannot see them.

Yes, you can see the physical results with tears of happiness or sadness, or of the feeling of joy with laughter and elation or an angry outburst with a scrunched-up face purple with rage. These are triggered by thought energy from the mind. What is faster than the speed of light? Answer: the speed of thought. It is thought energy that generates and channels your intuition. It is that feeling in your gut that makes you uneasy or sends a signal of warning to your body from your mind. Think of a loved one or favourite thing or place or pet and they are instantly in your mind. No delay, bang, they're there in perfect focus and clarity, no need to take a breath, the image is right in front of you.

Consciousness and conscience are spiritual. Jiminy Cricket from Walt Disney's *Pinocchio* had the mantra: 'Always let your conscience be your guide.' It is that silent voice steering you on the right path. It's up to you whether you take the advice, but sure enough, it is your best friend, your spiritual guide making an entrance into your thoughts. That brings me to another talent we all share. We are all psychic. Our psyche is our mind, our deepest thoughts. Being psychic is being Spirit. Our core identity.

Healing is your everyday evidence of this talent. Sending a smile, giving a hug, giving encouragement to someone, sends healing and shares our humanity with others. It can turn someone away from a negative path. Spiritual healing projects waves of comfort to soothe a physical, emotional or mental issue. Mediums can connect and heal by the power of thought alone.

Never forget that you are special. Embrace your spirituality. Discover more about yourself and celebrate what you reveal.

Coming Next

*The Realms of Spirit*

> *'Within the spiritual realms, you have another realm where the animals are, but in fact, it is all side by side within the ether.'*

Those are the words of Black Feathers and our tantalising introduction to the second half of the book – The Realms of Spirit. Are you ready to go deeper?

# PART TWO

## Spirit Side Chapters

# Eight

## The Realms of Spirit

Your Spirit ascends. Spiritually, you don't die. You evolve. This world, this planet, this earth, is a staging point on your spiritual way. This mortal life is but a pause on your upward ascent. You already exist within the spiritual realms. You are as one with the universe. A child of the universe.

Let's recap.

We've stated the principal task of Mediums is to provide evidence that spiritual life continues after physical death. Clairvoyance is their tool, their instrument. This gift is open to all, including the followers of different religions and faith groups. And with practice and dedication, to those on a spiritual path, broadly termed spiritualism. Connection is made with kindred spirits who have gone on before. Their continued presence sings out.

Additionally, there are channelled contributions from a number of Spirit Guides to help us understand our passage. This one was printed in *Believe in Spirit.* It is breathtaking. It's from 'The Scribe', an energy from within the realms, from within the Halls of Learning. It concerns the feeling of passing, of returning finally a wonderful description of the Homeland.

We've repeated this piece in case you haven't read *Believe in Spirit.*

*The Departure:*

*My body lay there with every fibre of my being crying out to be released. Thoughts in my head resembling some kind of prayer. Was I actually praying, did I pray before this pain racked my body?*

*A voice. There is a voice I can hardly hear; it is soothing, comforting and strangely relaxing. First, the words make no sense then the whispering starts. It's like something that is only heard by you and only you. The voice gets louder but not loud that it is bothersome. 'Don't be afraid; come with us, your time has come.'*

*A hand. I think it's a hand, it looks like a hand but then no, it's the shape of a hand being formed from the purest of light. It touches my mind then the unbelievable happens. My body is free from pain. I'm floating above my body and wish myself goodbye. My loved ones cry. My voice says, 'Please don't cry, I'm happy to go, it's my time.' But then, of course, they do not hear my words because there are no words, only my thoughts.*

*I find myself as high as I could ever have imagined, feeling as light as the lightest feather, the colours resembling the colours of the rainbow but in the deepest and brightest hue. Is this real? I pinch myself. No pain, no touch, no body, no eyes to see, no voice to speak, no ears to hear, yet all those sensations I can still achieve. My mind is whirring, my thoughts go back to the body I had just left, I can't get in, it has done its journey, it is finished with. My mind is now free.*

*Then something magical happened. My thoughts were filled with love and are directed straight to the loved one who is standing there looking over my, now lifeless, body. My only thought is to fill that person with this new love that is surrounding me. It is like sending out a light mist to surround that bereaved person; it floats and surrounds their aura. They slightly shudder and then I know my work is done. I have sent my love in all its purity.*

*My new journey will begin.*

*The Return:*

*Here is my Spirit, elevated into nothingness. Everything that is in the surrounding area is the finest, most delicate mist. I can see, but can I see? There is nothing there, only this purest mist. I can hear, but what do I hear? There is no noise but this very subtle hum. It's like nothing I have experienced when my soul and physical body were attached. This is pure peace, with the lightest of touch that you cannot feel, but it is there. The only way I can explain it is if you are floating amongst the finest and softest feathers.*

*There is the subtlest hum surrounding my thoughts. The noise I hear has no sound but words are spoken through thoughts. It is my family joining my energies to welcome me back to the Homeland. My thoughts are filled with love and gratitude for the welcome party for my return. They whisper and float around my energies with the purest of love. 'You are home, you are safe. We welcome you back.'*

*There is so much love surrounding my energies a desire comes upon me to distribute this love back to my loved ones who have been left behind. How do I do this? Think. What should I do? Then my mind remembers them feeling sad at my parting, that's when the words come back to me; the soundless words that could not be spoken, only the thought, 'Don't be sad, be happy for me.' I remember them. It was through my thought processes that I sent the energy directly their way. Then a feeling like that of a warm glow, floats away and is directed once again to the ones who have been left behind.*

*Now my thoughts are whirring; this is happening, this is achievable. I am actually able to make contact with those who are still on the earth. We may be divided by the veil between the two worlds but we can actually connect through our thought waves. My energies want to clap, skip, dance and laugh with happiness at the thought that, although we are separated by the physical, we are still connected by our minds.*

The Homeland:

*I've heard tales of the Homeland, tales of wonder, tales of peace and love, tales of the purity of the return, tales of everlasting existence, tales which were unbelievable, too many to absorb and believe. Did I believe? My mind is now racing away with thoughts tumbling over and over of how stories were building up in my mind of the departure and the return.*

*My thoughts are settling down now to the discovery that my energies are actually back within the Realms of Spirit, secure within the pure love you can only experience when back in our world. Clarity is beginning to dawn upon me. My mind becomes aware of what has just gone before me, of my departure from the earth to the return and arrival back in the Homeland. How quickly we forget about the security of the Homeland once we have allowed our soul to be secured again within a physical body, to become a person who walks and dwells upon the earth, to try to make a difference to those who will walk alongside of us. That is over for my Spirit now.*

*The eternal life of which you hear about is here within these realms, within our thoughts. My Spirit will now start upon the long and joyous journey of evolving towards the purity of the light, towards reconciling with the Creator, the giver of all. It is spoken on your earth that, once you reach the realms, Judgement Day will be there waiting. For a physical being to hear these words, the thoughts can conjure up fear and anxiety of what is to be before you. This prospect waits for me now. It is my time to go through the catalogue of my lifetime. To see my life flash before me with every flaw, disturbances, thoughtless acts, sadness, joy, achievements, love, misery, happiness, humility towards others. It is a time of reckoning and of understanding how we coped with our emotions that made up who we were. How we treated ourselves, and more importantly, how we treated others.*

*It is said that God forgives all. It is God that helps and guides you along the road to reconciliation of your own self; how to learn from your previous existence, how to forgive yourself, and to help you cleanse your soul for your journey towards the eternal light. During all these happenings, my mind will now have to learn how to live without a body. To adjust to being just a Spirit with thoughts that can be compared to living a life on the earth. The difference being is that our thoughts are not marred by the material or the physicality that is experienced on the earth. Our thoughts, in time, become purified and our one aim is to direct that love and purity back towards those who we have left behind, to confirm to them that we have only left them in body but are still very alive much within our thoughts.*

*On communication to our loved ones, we have a glimpse of the sadness they are feeling through the suffering of their loss for us. This increases our love and, by using the full power of thought, we can envelop them within the love and light of Spirit and hope that eventually this power of thought will be able to encase them within our warm glow and hopefully reduce their sadness.*

Would you agree that we tend to think of the realms as a separate world, perhaps as Heaven? A world somewhere in outer space or a mystical place beyond our imagining? Blue Mountain spoke of 'Heaven' in these terms:

*I want to speak about our world. The world that you are all going to come back to and that you would have inhabited at one time. When people imagine our world, they imagine a big round ball like a planet. Our world is not like that. It is not a planet it is in the ether. It is the air that is all around you. We are in the ether and all around you. It's like another world that you cannot see or touch. There is so much activity within that realm. People may speak of the different levels or realms. They are there, they exist. Everything is done through the mind, through the thought. I'm not telling you anything that you haven't heard before.*

*When Mediums are speaking of our world, they like to visualise it. They would say there are buildings, there are houses, there are universities, green grass and flowers. It is because everything has to have meaning and understanding to allow you to link in and understand about our world and the difference between our world and yours.*

*The worlds are a replica of one another. You are in a material world the other one is visions within the mind. We describe certain visions when we come through to make it real, to help you understand what we are talking about. It is important that the reader can read it with clarity. There are always people who want to dig and poke what other people have written. In order that these people will not be able to find any blemishes with any words or phrases you have put down, we want you to mention the Halls of Learning, everything is done through the mind.*

Emmanuel added these words channelled by Suzi Cartwright during a meeting on 25 April 2022:

*I'll give you a secret, my friends. There are no golden gates. Man has created it. It is just a vision. Hundreds of years ago, someone thought in their infinite wisdom that if we should create a world called Heaven and that a departed soul would be met at the golden gates by angels and cherubs. This idea is planted in your mind to give comfort and consolation, so when you come up to the realms, a key to the golden gate to Heaven will be turned.*

*There is no gate. And no pit of Hell. Every energy gets sifted through. You all get sorted into certain categories where you need to go. Before you reach that point, it is important that you keep mind, body and soul intact as much as you possibly can. You need to go forward in life. If your body isn't 100 per cent, you will find it a struggle and you could start to blame everyone else because they will say, 'It is that person's fault that I am the way I am.' It is your own responsibility to do this check on yourself every now and again. So, you should go on in the most positive way you can.*

*It is important to keep your family close to you. And, my friends, I have got a family here with me today (Janet's family). I have her dear daughter and her partner and they are sitting side by side. They are here and they have their arms around each other to give her the strength to carry on the pathway we have placed her. As she is here to make as much difference as Suzi, and Jayne and Stephen to make a difference in their own lives.*

*It is unusual for us to do this but we thought we would show that although these are gone in body, they are very much here in Spirit.*

To continue in the same vein, here are the words of Tomahawk during a meeting on 8 May 2023:

*I'm going to depict the spiritual world. You have your buildings and streets. The buildings are very high, as are the Halls of Learning. We do not reside in dwellings or homes because we do not need to rest because the energy is in its purest forms. With the architecture, you could imagine it to be in the twelfth century in Europe or evoke the English universities of Oxford and Cambridge. They would be set down in stones as they are such a wonderment. When you go into the halls and the rooms, you would get lost because of all the knowledge. When you step outside into the clear air you will see the green of the grass, the vegetation, the trees and flowers because this is what people could see in their minds. The colours are everything you would see in your earth plane is magnified.*

*This is what people see when they close their minds and meditate. We can make this happen in people's minds. They like to see the animals all well fed and nurtured. No animal will ever be ill-treated, as they are pure energy. I want people to feel they could touch the tranquillity and comfort like the softness of cotton wool.*

Spirit is simply saying that Heaven or the realms can be anything your imagination wants it to be, to look like the pictures in your mind or to function in a way that pleases you. The spiritual realms are never-ending. They are the embodiment of a celestial magnitude almost beyond our consciousness.

It is possible to conceive of an invisible world in which new spiritual energies are created and progress through repeated incarnations until they become pure and as one with the Creator.

There's one thing we can be sure of and that's the Dark Side. For the first time in our writings, Spirit wanted us to talk about the Dark Side. We will explore why this negative balance persists in Chapter Eleven.

### *Incarnation – A Reminder*

Guiding Light joined us on 14 November 2022 to remind us of the cycle of incarnation.

*Good evening, my friends, I come with love and protection*

*from the spiritual realms. The divine light is shining above your heads. It is a pleasure to come to speak to you. Our world is like no other world. We are pure energy, it is nothingness, it is like looking into a deep void. You will know that there is something there. You will know from your world with the mist and the fog, you look into it and just see shadows. This is how some people envision our world. Except there are no shadows. We have our minds, our thought processes within this invisible pod of energy which is impossible to kill. Listen to the words I say, as there is a need to speak about the invisibility of the spiritual realms.*

*We are a Collective of multiple energies, millions and billions of energies. At times these energies can condense into the one. It is previous incarnations that people have had. When people imagine the spiritual realms, they think of different categories in people's minds. One is of their loved ones and friends, their acquaintances, so a very small pocket of energies within their minds. For others, they would be able to envision every living soul who has ever been on the earth. When you go back to the realms, all the energies are jampacked into the ether. We speak about the energies moving on or moving up inside the realms, people can't imagine or get out of their minds that the atmosphere around them is jampacked with energies.*

*I want to say these next words very carefully. You have the Sunflower. You start off with one seed. Imagine you have a flower of one pod. We are going back thousands and thousands of years. I'm saying this so you can get clarification of what you want to write in your next book. Imagine the first pod that started out as a spiritual being that went into an earthly incarnation. When that first person's life finished their incarnation, they would have come back to the spiritual realms. It would have learnt much and it would have had a choice of either going back to the earth to have another life to see what you can accomplish in another life. Then another second seed is sown. That energy would just come back, it could be two years or three hundred years. That second seed would forget about anything that happened in its previous incarnation. The first incarnation would start its journey back in the realms, it would be making its way back to the pod from whence it came. It would not be losing any of its identity because, as I said to you in a previous message, your soul would have the fragment of the memory of your identity. It stays there in the soul and begins to move on.*

*Then we come back to the second incarnation. When that second person comes back to the realms, they also start to come back into the realms; it just lays there and in people's memories for ever and ever. It is only in people's memories while they are still on the earth.*

*It is needed in your memory while you are on the earth. It is only important to have that memory in your heart, and your heart is aching because that person has left. You have to learn how to manage your emotions after that person has left. The memories are only needed while they are on the earth. When they come back, those memories are released. You are aware that when you come back you are with the energies of all the people you have met on the earth during that incarnation.*

*The second energy will start to follow the footsteps of the first energy and start ascending up to the divine light.*

*On the way, many energies decide to remain within the realms. Through that journey is a journey like no other because you can go into the Halls of Learning. There is no conception of time over here, we are in a place where time means nothing but we have to speak in terms of time so that you can understand it. The previous energy that would have come from that pod would have started its ascent to the divine light. So, you have a trail of energies following one another. The identification of that person is laid out there and is never forgotten so that people will be able to make contact.*

Each incarnation and each return is a learning experience. A progression. These words are from Cheyenne, recorded on 29 September 2023, to continue the conversation.

*We bring much energy and greetings from our world. It is something we like to hear. Come, brother, come forward and speak about your world. We can go deep within the echelons of your world. We can go up higher and higher and delve deeper and deeper within all the planes and spheres that are here. People do not always understand this. They talk about levels. They say there are seven levels in the spiritual realms. What they don't realise is that within each level there is a vastness of black denseness. They don't realise it is the lightest and happiest place that you can live. These spheres and planes are there for each and every energy to rest upon so they can learn what life is all about when you come back to the spiritual realms.*

*Because the rest of their energy that has been before them is evolving up into another sphere or it could be on the same sphere but in a different plane. Is it a race to catch up with the rest of your energy? Of course not, my friend. That is not on the mind of any newly returned Spirit or ones that have been here for hundreds of years. There is no need to catch up with the rest of that energy that is veering towards the divine light. It is there because each and every one of you have choices and your own journeys when you come back to the Realms of Spirit. You can go into all different pockets of the areas of where you are so you can learn and embellish what you have learnt or understood on the earth plane. You can focus on certain things and many of the energies here or many of the energies that touch your energy or those who are conversing now or will be conversing in the future.*

*We are all here learning within the depths of the spiritual realms. People often speak about our world. Our world, as you know, is within the ether, it is nothingness. Within that nothingness, there is billions and billions of buildings and Halls of Learning. There is so much there as it is all done within the thoughts of Spirit within the ether. All these thoughts are in your mind when you come back to Spirit. Your Spirit rises back into the ether, it dissipates, it is all around you. Billions and billions of thoughts that would have been in the minds of the spirits who have walked on your earth. When we come through, people like to hear about our world, so for people to understand, we have to put it in a way that it relates to the world you are living in.*

*To help you understand I can say that now that I was living in a reservation. I would have been with people I loved and felt comfortable with. People who would have understood the earth, the sky, the trees, the animals, everything that was all around us. Often people say that I am speaking from the Cheyanne tribe and this is why I put that name into the mix. We would not have done anything to harm or affect the earth. If we had to kill anything, we would have used every particle. I can put my mind back. I can say I am on the reservation and the sky is quite blue and we have started to prepare ourselves for the up-and-coming winter.*

*All of a sudden you are getting a picture in your mind. We would have to place our tepees and living quarters in parts where there was vegetation and trees to stop the winds from destroying us. If you walked out of that space there would be nothingness, it would be like a desert. I could then switch and say that I was another energy, a monk in Tibet, and I could describe it as very mountainous and cold, but in the spring, we get warmth and vegetation. You get the image of a monastery. I could go on. This is how our world is. We can direct our energies to every person who is listening to us. We have to think very quickly on our feet.*

People talk about the seven levels of the spiritual realms. The highest being the connection with the godhead, the Creator, the supreme being. They mention the planes and the spheres within each level. These are all invisible nothingness, a part of the infinite structure of the spiritual universe. We do know the ultimate aim of our Spirit constantly progressing until a divine state of purity is attained. This progression over time is part spent learning and development within the realms.

The second is the personal programme of incarnation and subsequent reincarnation on earth. This is the spiritual assault course of mind, body and emotions on earth during each visit to challenge our being.

### *Heaven, Hell and the Realms*

The religious concept of Hell depicted as a place of suffering and punishment is not part of the spiritual realms. There is no Hell in Heaven. Hell is here on earth. Just think of all the wars and suffering.

Grey Dove put it like this:

> *We know from your conversations, Stephen, when you speak of Heaven and Hell, and in many times from Janet's mouth. It is from Heaven where all the peace is and Hell is where there is much disharmony and destruction. Your world oozes destruction. There are many people dying in horrific circumstances and through many wars. There are so much horrific things happening in your world. If there was a Hell, it would be where you are living. When you approach the subject of Hell, this is how we would like you to write about it. We have always been there to help with the pages of your book. We have given you the information to put it in or to tweak it.*
>
> *We are not the authors. If I was the author and writing on the subject of Heaven and Hell. Hell is a place where no one would want to live if they had a choice. The world in which you live is made up of many people with different personalities, many dispositions, many thoughts on how they would want*

*to run their lives and how they want to run other people's lives. People would remain in the pockets of their countries to fight for peace and get rid of the Hell that has been brought upon them. And to get rid of the person who is wielding the Ball of Power. The Ball of Power can cause much destruction but on the other hand it can cause good. But all the good it can cause is minute compared to all the destruction.*

*If I was to continue on the subject of Hell, I would also integrate other words as Hell is also a place where a person can be living within their mind if it is not functioning properly or the choices they make, can cause them to go on a different path. Hell can be living in a body at times where you cannot climb out.*

*We are in Heaven. It is a world that has been given to somewhere of peace and free of any pain. Free of any trauma and full of peace and love. We are always there within your body and your soul.*

As we write, the Ball of Power is in the hands of tyrants and dictators with wars in Ukraine, the Middle East and Sudan. Territorial wars and drug wars never end.

There's one other question that's hanging in the air. What happens when those guilty of causing evil die? Or people who have abused or seduced the Ball of Power or are guilty of despicable crimes? How are they treated?

As spiritual beings, when their lives end, they will return to the realms like you and me. At that point they will look back over their lives and review their 'Book of Life'. Their Spirit will be held in a dense area of energy, in suspension for time without end. Until they realise the harm they've caused and plea for forgiveness. That is as closest to Hell as the spiritual realms get. It is for the individual energy to accept responsibility for their actions in this life before they have a hope of eventually moving on. I guess it's the equivalent of spiritual solitary confinement where people who have committed crimes like Hitler and Putin have to finally face their heartlessness. It's an eternity where their minds replay in sharp detail the traumas they've caused. Until they see the light of contrition.

As Grey Dove says, it is a pity there are few who use the Ball of Power for good purposes.

### *Astral Travelling*

Before we leave these descriptions of the realms. There's another aspect you may have heard of, it's astral travelling. This is when someone has a spiritual out-of-body (OBE) experience. It is not linked to a physical trauma like being involved in an accident or lying in hospital. It is being taken on a spiritual adventure. This is how Spirit describes the sensation:

> *People who do astral travelling will be aware of the vivid colouring and images when you're travelling around in the astral planes. It is likened to the spiritual planes but it is not. It is not part of the spiritual realms. If you went over the white light there would be no return. If you do go into the astral plane there will be a return because you are having an out-of-body experience.*
>
> *This happens when you are in your sleep state when your guardians, your angels, whoever you have there with you*

*take you mentally out of your body and they will take you around the astral planes. In the astral world, you will envision this for yourself and witness what is happening. At times the most sensitive of people need to be taken out of their own inner body. They can just feel that lightness all around them. They can feel free from their body that's living in the material world. It is that light relief people feel when they have that experience.*

*Your soul leaves your body for a very short time that's when they have experience of the astral plane. They hold on to the memory. They feel they have been travelling all night but they haven't. They've only been travelling for a minute or two but that vividness is etched within their mind. It is the freedom they feel from leaving their physical body and travel around in the atmosphere.*

In Chapter Ten of *Believe in Spirit* Rosie recalled two of her astral travelling experiences. Here is a more recent memory:

*My guide telepathically told me that we are not the only soul who return to the Spirit realms. He told me the universe is vast and that we are not the only ones living in this vast space. He told me that there are people, animals and planets that exist and have existed long before us and continue to exist in our time.*

*I saw this amazing animal. It had two toes, with claws like a sloth. It had a super large head with, I presume, four eyes because I saw two on the one side of its head that I could see. The eyes were bigger than a rhino or elephant eyes.*

Let's return to what the Realms of Spirit look like:
Grey Dove continues: What the realms look like.

*I want to get back, my friend, to what the gentleman asked of what the spiritual realms look like. You often hear of the Halls of Learning, we speak about the Sisters of Mercy within their hospitals, we speak about many people and what they are doing. They are preparing things for you back on the earth. All this is done with mind and thought.*

*For the person on the earth, they can imagine what they want it to look like. You can get many pictures in your mind as what you want it to be. Blue sky, green grass and the sun continually shining. The animals are there because the animals are a major part of the spiritual world because the animals have, like you humans, they live within a physical body of the species they were born into. Anything with a beating heart comes back to the spiritual realms.*

*People want to imagine what they think Heaven is. They think this is where their loved ones go when they come back. When the time comes for them to cut the cords of their physical being. It is up to you how you depict what the spiritual realms look like. It is personal and different for everyone. Some don't see it as a world. They see it within their memories, within their minds, as they have proof given to them. To many people, it is very important to picture something to where they are going to go or where their loved ones are waiting.*

*If someone loses a child, it is very important to know their child has gone to the Sisters of Mercy or to the angels and that they are living in a gold or sunny-like place where the children continue to play in laughter. And that their elderly parents are in a place that is peaceful and restful. They like to see them in their armchairs in a peaceful atmosphere. It is a very personal thing.*

*When we speak about the Halls of Learning, it is natural to envision them like our colleges and universities on earth because it's the only thing that makes sense to you. When you go inside there are rooms of different sizes where people are being taught. That's why you can easily think of what the Halls of Learning look like.*

## Blog

### *The Book of Life*

Your book of life lies open for you to complete.

Every moment, every experience, every emotional high and low are sealed within those pages. They tell the story of the decisions we took, the sadness and joy and the way we cared for others and cared for the world around us. Moments of loving bliss are captured in each timeline. We came into this world as pure of Spirit, a clean spiritual slate if you like. All that has happened from that first birth cry onwards has shaped your soul. Your soul holds the spiritual and emotional log of this life's journey. Your soul records your spiritual progression. Has it evolved? What did you learn? What are you learning now?

The point of living this life is simple. It is to live and

progress spiritually. You may have nodded in agreement as you read those first words.

Pause a moment. Ask yourself, what did those words really mean? Your brain sorted them out and made a kind of comfortable sense. The real meaning is so immense, so incredible, it's almost impossible to comprehend. If you thought life was a one-time experience, a one-off one-way trip to the material world with a straight line ending in nothingness, you'd be wrong. The truth bends your mind into shapes and reaches conclusions you will barely believe. It is the unbelievable truth. In spiritual terms, you are immortal.

Life is eternal. This life is just one station on your way. As the final chapters of this life close, your soul ascends and returns to the world of Spirit. Your spiritual life continues. The lives of loved ones you've lost are continuing too. They are walking along their path. You are walking along yours.

What happens then?

Life continues. You revert to an entity of energy, of thought energy. Your mind faces the challenge of living without a body. This is how Running Water, a Navajo spiritual guide, described the sensations.

*Imagine you have no body. Your eyes are closed and you are floating in the air. All around you is extreme peace and you feel no weight at all. Suddenly you want to walk, to place your feet on the floor. There is no floor. You are in the air. You put your arms out to help you stand. There is nothing for you to hold on to.*

*You are surrounded by nothingness. This is an example to help you understand. Don't worry. You would automatically open your eyes and immediately come back into a physical perception of your surroundings in your mind.*

*The Spirit would not feel distressed or alarmed only slightly disorientated at first as to how they can operate in this existence without a body. Through the power of thought they would still be able to walk, talk, run, jump, dance, sing and continue to 'do' whatever they would have done on the earth. They just have to think it and it will happen. Straight away.*

*Life in Spirit continues and so does your own learning and development. We all continue to progress. Your mind is where the action is, the dynamic action of thought. Living in the spiritual world means you no longer have to worry about material restrictions, there are no physical constraints. You are free of the pull of gravity. You are lighter than a feather surrounded by peace and light.*

## Coming Next

### *The Dark Side*

We can't ignore the Dark Side. It's the powerful force of negativity that surrounds us, created and fed by anger and hate. It infects the planet and pollutes the skies above us. It's sustained by jealousy, greed, anger, hatred and a lust for power. The counter energy of love and light is our response.

# Nine

## The Dark Side

*Light vs Dark*

We've spoken about Spirit in a loving and positive way. At the same time, there's no denying there's a darker side to life. This is the first time Spirit wanted us to discuss this topic. Our earthly experience is a melding of two forces. We are continually faced with challenges of right and wrong, good and bad. The Dark Side supplies that challenge in our personal decision making. It is how we respond that shapes our moods and either supports or soothes our anxieties. The direction, the choice, is ours alone.

You feel it too. If you're angry and shouting, the emotional electricity created becomes a physical force. It exudes from you, dispersing and rising into the atmosphere. It is an invisible force, a weapon of negative energy, a shadow entity of darkness within us.

One of Michael's guides put it like this:

*A lot of people think the Dark Side does not exist. The best way to think about it is to think of shadows. Think about light to know there's an opposite as well. When we look at the sun there is a shadow behind us. A shadow is always there. We always cast a shadow. There are energies on the other side of love and joy. People think there is light but not energies that are pulling people into the space of darkness. This plays out in terms of addictions, low self-worth, anxiety and suicidal thoughts, anything that is a heavy weight is where the darker energies play.*

*In order for us to alleviate this, and go through life in a higher vibration, we need to understand other energies are in place. Our job is to show how there are greater elements of fulfilment: health, wealth and happiness. The darker side will play tricks on us to stop us gaining fulfilment. By doing things on a higher vibration with no expectations, we rise above it. Inevitably, we will find there are opposites that draw us back. The twin forces of energy are cause and effect, good and evil. The higher you go spiritually, the darker side of energy threatens and needs to be acknowledged and overcome. Light overcomes darkness.*

To continue the flow, here are the words of Brown Bear. He was one of our first guides and a member of the Native American Indian Group of Eight. It was recorded on 4 September 2023. He raised the issue of the Dark Side:

*There is a darker side to the spiritual world. If you go to other countries, they embellish upon this. They have many different names for it. People believe in the Dark Side and it puts fear into them like witchcraft; they are elementals, they are all tuning into the negative energies. They can manipulate their minds and embellish upon it and use it as a weapon to put the fear in many people. And it is being said in the churches and centres and homes they should send out healing to those who need it and send out the white light of love. If people have the wrong intentions, they can reverse where that energy is going, it can have the reverse effect upon people.*

*It's a build-up of negativity. If you have negative and positive, black and white, people always think about the positive side of the spiritual world. They never think about the negative or Dark Side because they think it doesn't exist. Imagine you have a large round sphere; it is all light and bright and where all the love is. But on the edges, you have that rim of darkness where the good energies are constantly warding off the build-up of negativity that goes all round the globe. For people who have lopsided dedication, they can use it not for good but for mischievous deeds or fear. It all goes back to the fear and the power. When people have power in their hands, they always want to use it as a weapon. This is why we have chosen this subject this evening.*

This piece from Emmanuelle, recorded on 6 March 2023, focuses on our state of mind, whether it involves mental illness or other pressures we have to deal with every day. It's a great insight into the care and understanding from our Spirit Guides to our pressures they pick up on.

*What's the saying on your earth? Through the darkness comes the light? When the light is there, sometimes it is hard for people to keep it there. There are fears that the darkness is going to come and smother them again. People on the earth have your minds. When you're in Spirit, your mind is pure. It has been cleansed and filled with knowledge.*

*On the earth, the mind can be impaired. At times many people are inflicted with darker thoughts and lots of confusion. It is all down to mental illness because it is a mental block that can affect people. It can affect any one of them here. People get so confused and full of dark thoughts that they have to take their own life so they can get back into the light. You do not have to take your own life to get you into the light. You can get back into the light by believing, relaxing, just trying to allow all these dark thoughts to go out of your head.*

*When people have a physical illness people can send out their thoughts to them, give them their sympathy, their empathy, and they will tell them that they are sorry for their plight. But when someone has a mental illness to the extent that they are causing havoc or mental distress, people do not send out sympathy or empathy or love and protection. They just walk away from that person as that person is creating negative energy. So, you would say for that person to relax and send their energy into the light? Within their mind they may think they are consumed with so much darkness they've forgotten what the lightness was ever like. They've forgotten that the lightness can lift them up. It is very difficult for them to get back within the light.*

*When these people come back to Spirit, they are so appreciative of being out of that body because that mind, those thoughts, would have been in that physical body in which they have been incarnated. It would be a defect that made their thoughts and their brains work and act in that way. Once the Spirit has gone, they would be back to normal because the impairment they had has been left behind. This is a very difficult subject to talk about as when you are talking about mental illness, people think that it is within the mind and thoughts as it is an impairment in certain parts of the brain that help to function the body. When the soul has left the body, the brain is not of any use anymore and the body is left behind.*

*When these spirits have left the body, the spirits are so pleased that they are back in the light they wish to make it their work, their duty to help people who have mental illnesses upon the earth.*

*Therefore, how do you help the person on the earth who has been filled, so consumed with darkness, how do you help them who have suffered with depression, fatigue, from thoughts that they are disliked by everyone else? How do you help them get back into the light? The light is always there. Especially as to their way of thinking, they are being covered in the darkness.*

*This is a defect in the brain, it is nothing to do with the spiritual energies. Do you understand where I am going with this?*

*You will meet people at certain times who will ask you certain questions, especially people who do not believe or who call themselves cynical or sceptics. They want proof all the time. They say they believe in these spirits or ghosts. Bring me these spirits, bring me these ghosts, can you prove that? They will be asking why did this happen or why did that happen; sometimes people want to place you in the corner to tie you up. They do not share your beliefs. These people are cynical in their own minds, their own thoughts. Whether you say you are believing in the spiritual world or Christian or Muslim or Hindu, they will always want to trick you. The only way you can reply to people is to have love in my heart and the love is always shining. The darkness sometimes overtakes but it is like the sun going over the clouds, it doesn't mean the sun has disappeared. When the clouds have gone, the sun comes back. The same can be said of the lightness, the brightness. Mental illness is real. It is a physical ailment because it has been treated in the brain. You can only send out your loving thoughts to people who suffer so. It is like purgatory inside their minds. To be encased within the darkness for a long time can bring everyone down. It is something to be in the light.*

*This separated the physical and mental side of things. Spirit is mind, thought and energy. You are governed by what you say, but the energy around you is keeping your soul very much alive. With all the spiritual working while you are on the earth, the workings inside your brain. If things are not knitted correctly, they are going to affect how the person's mind is working. The minute that energy is erased from that physical body then that mind goes back to living in the light again.*

*In preparation for our meetings, you should sit quietly and shed all the hustle and bustle around you in the daytime. People need to get in tune with their own selves, or in tune with their spiritual energies, and with the Mediums they've used. She has never done that. She (Janet) sits down and allows us to rest within their auric field. Then we can speak on any subject without being tainted. It is a lesson to many people. We applaud people who read books and garner all the knowledge they can. But when they are working in this capacity it is very easy to allow things to come from their own minds from things they've read previously or they've listened to. When we work with her, everything that is being said has not come from her mind, it has come from ours.*

### *Hauntings Ghosts and Elementals*

There are hauntings and ghosts. The difference is film and television programmes tend to put a fearful spin on their existence for entertainment purposes. This is not always the case. A haunting can be by a caring, beneficial energy. The presence could be the result of a deep commitment to a time, place or family. It could also be the result of an energy needing help to move on.

We would like to mention that the existence of dark energies are sometimes called elementals. This can be confusing in that these negative energies are of a spiritual nature and not the four natural elements of Fire, Water, Earth and Air. These are energies created by negativity. They sense and react to stress, anxiety, despair and depression. The waves of unhappiness and hopelessness shape their mischief. It may help to envision these invisible, malignant energies as solid spherical beings.

They multiply on a diet of disillusionment along with mental and physical distress. In the same way light, joy, and happiness are our powerful responses. Elementals are fuelled by depression. When you're feeling low, out-think the heaviness by tapping into an uplifting memory. Run that video of upliftment in your head and blow those clouds and the elementals away.

There are two words ever-present in this book: mind and thought. This is the communication channel between Spirit and ourselves. As we are spirits in human form, there is a union of blended consciousness. Thoughts and minds become as one. Human and Spirit form a spiritual connection between our two worlds. This union is the active co-operation between two sets of spiritual beings. As you will read in the next chapter.

## Blog

*A Poem from Spirit*

The beautiful hummingbird is Josiah's symbol. Josiah is a Spirit

Guide who lived in Virginia in the southern states of America 150 years ago. He is an important member of the group of guides who are inspiring our work here on earth today. Josiah is a writer and poet. He takes great delight in crafting poems for people who would benefit from a deeply personal message written only for them.

The love and learning from Spirit are evident in every line. Spirit is within every one of us. Think of Spirit as friends. They were once on earth. They were like us. We are like them. They were real people. They retain their personality in Spirit as we will when we pass.

Here is an uplifting poem from Josiah:

**Your Light Shines**

Your light shines like a beacon of hope
Your light is like a hundred dancers
They jump and turn like diamonds in the water
You glow from your soul

You give your heart to all
You ask nothing in return
You help those who fall
You give all you have

Your soul is cleansed
Your soul is blessed
Your mind is clear to pave the way
So others can follow the light

Close your eyes, my dear sweet soul
And envision your spiritual friends

With lanterns in hands to guide you along
Your path is waiting

The door is opened wide
Walk through into the lake of wisdom
And drink in all that is waiting
We are there with you on your journey
Come, follow us, we will guide you on your earth's journey
To help those who cannot help themselves.

## Coming Next

*Soul Rescue*

There's a crucial service that earthbound Mediums perform for Spirit. Soul Rescue. It occurs when someone passes into Spirit under extreme, unexpected circumstances. In the most part violent. In the next chapter we'll describe the role Mediums play.

# Ten

# Soul Rescue

*Soul Rescue Explained by Spirit*

*Running Water's Soul Rescue Message – 18 March 2021*

Running Water explains how a tiny fragment of a soul is detached in a violent passing. The fragment is wrenched away in a cataclysmic instant. The main body of the soul reaches the realms. The role of the Medium is to help reconnect the fragment to make the soul whole again.

Mediums work alongside lightworker energies in Spirit to fulfil this task.

*I would like to explain about the energies you work with and the lightworkers. It is like they are in that part of the world that can be called a 'no-man's-land'. The majority of their energy is back within our world, a fragment of them got disconnected when they had a sudden passing. Every energy that you bring over is a sudden or traumatic passing that they had to endure while they were on the earth. When a person passes it is like a shock and so sudden that they feel they are still around on the earth. When you speak about the Soul Rescue, it is like part of their memory that has been left behind and needs to be married up with the rest.*

*We have a lightworker here and they want to intervene.*

*Hello, my friends, first of all I would like to thank you on behalf of myself and all the other lightworkers who are within our realms for delivering the lost souls back into the Homelands. It is very traumatic for many of these energies. It is like their soul being ripped from their body and the cord being broken, the silver cord that connects the spiritual cord that links the soul to the body together. You can imagine it being torn and not sure whether they have passed or still on earth. They can be there for many years, for hundreds of years, as you know. There are many of us in the spiritual realms; we are there on the peripheral edge to welcome these souls back to the spiritual realms so they can lay back with the rest of their soul. We have no conception of time in their 'no-man's-land' or in the Realms of Spirit. The souls may have been in limbo for hundreds of years, or two months or ten months, who knows. The job you are doing is very important because you are helping the whole of their spiritual energy to become whole and rest in peace. I know there will be questions in your mind. Because the whole Spirit has not been together, does that hold back the energy in Spirit? Yes, my friend, it does hold them back until they are whole again and develop and go up to the divine light. The rest of the Spirit would have rested until they are reconnected with the lost fragment. There is another question that is in your mind, 'Why is it that they cannot get re-entry to our world? Why do they need lightworkers and others on the world to rescue them and bring them back?' Can I answer this, my friend?*

*It is because of the trauma of their passing they have found themselves lost within the ether and because they have no conception of time, there are many there; it is very busy, my friend. I can see them. They are queueing up; there are too many of them for you to rescue this evening. But we wait; as you know, they have no conception of time, so they stand there and wait. They can see the light. They go to the madam, the lady (Rosie), because this is what you have been groomed for, my dear. This is what all your work for Spirit has been for. Spirit weaves all this light around you so energies can see you and know that this is a safe place as they step into your energy. If you had not come across 'our gift' (Janet) here you would have had to set up your own little group with other people. And you would have passed them over by saying prayers and saying go towards the light. We know that when they get into her light they will come back to Spirit immediately. We know that some people have lightworkers with them and they have to trust that the lightworker takes them back safely into our realms. This way that you are doing it is a very special way and it is a pure way to reunite the energies with their soul. It is like a wind that sucks up the energy into the ether, into the atmosphere and that spiritual energy stays there until the time is right for them to come back into the light.*

(Steve's question) How do they know when it's their time?

*As I say, my friend, it is a mass of dense energy in the atmosphere, like a feather that is floating; you can set a thousand feathers up into the wind and some would continuously float on and on and some would settle back down and fall back to the earth. There is no time limit. No klaxon will sound, there is no trumpet that will sound and call your name. They are just swirling around in the vortex they are in. It is like part of that energy has gone to sleep and suddenly it wakes up and comes alive again. Do not be sad for them. There is much sadness but that is due to their passings. You have a special gift, my dear, and, the gentleman, you are there to witness everything and be able to help deliver these spiritual energies back to their rightful place within our realms.*

*I'm going to go now. We don't normally come and converse, but I just felt I would because Running Water is concerned for his vessel. There is much protection around her. It demonstrates, my friend, that what you are doing is serious. And this is what many people forget when they are working with the spiritual energies.*

On 23 February 2024, Janet and I were in our normal Friday morning meeting with Spirit. I was writing this chapter on Soul Rescue, and there was a question I wanted to ask:

'What happens to those souls that remain while others are helped to reconnect in the realms?'

Running Water responded:

> *The fragments of energy that remain make their way towards the light. They have been helped over the years by Mediums who've meditated and generated the light to attract those souls. They learn to gravitate towards the light. In your world there are thousands upon thousands of people who do this work to help souls cross over. Eventually all the souls go over and are not stuck in limbo, they all go towards the light. The people who you've helped are very grateful.*

### *How do Rosie and Janet Begin Soul Rescue?*

Ordinarily in clairvoyance, a Medium would connect with Spirit and be in a 'ready to receive' mode. Within a short time, perhaps only seconds, Spirit will begin to 'transmit' information for the Medium to pass on.

With Soul Rescue, there's an extra step. In most meetings there are three of us involved. My role is to help create a calming atmosphere with silence and an opening prayer. Rosie and Janet connect with their guides. I keep my eyes open during the meeting as the girls enter a higher state of consciousness with eyes closed. I try to ensure there are no disturbances from phones or other distractions that will affect the sensitive energies that immediately increase within the room. Over the years, the girls have developed a way of working. Rosie would be the initial magnet with her spiritual light shining to attract lost souls. Often Janet would sense the energy quickly as they work in harmony.

Rosie would describe her first soul by their appearance and the circumstances of their passing. In the same instant, Janet would also connect with the energy. What happens next is astounding. Janet's bright light draws the visiting energy to cross the room, attracted to her aura. The rescue begins. The returning soul is drawn through the layers of her surrounding aura without brushing her physical body. She feels the rapid transfer happen. Janet jerks upwards as if she'd had an electric shock. The rescue is complete. The energy passes into the realms as a reunited soul.

Sometimes we learn the traumatic details of how these energies passed as they talk to us during the passing process. We'll share some of these now. The notes are fast-paced interactions between the girls using their initials.

### *Stories from the Soul Fragments*

The dates are of our meeting, not of the events and times portrayed in the stories. Let's begin.

#### *1. 1st July 2022 meeting notes.*

NFL American Football Star. We believe he played for the San Francisco 49ers as a lineman in 2005.

> *R: I've got a Black guy. He would have died on the field. It would have made the papers. He was known. He was wearing a white shirt and helmet he had stripes on it. He came in*

*strong with the whole kit and helmet with the grill. He's showing me his hair would have been an afro cut. He would have had a dark complexion, not deep black. It happened while he was still on the pitch in his kit. He's broad. A large African-American man.*

*J: He's taking his helmet off, he's sweating. It was very quick. It was very sudden. It was a heart attack. There was a lot of people around, a crowd watching the match. He just loved the game. It is as if a part of his memory is still there with the game. He thinks he let the team down. That thought kept that particle of energy separate from the rest of his soul. He felt he should have done his health checks. He's passed into Spirit. He's gone.*

2. *A little boy drowns in a pond.*

*R: I can see a white bunny. It's being chased by a little boy.*

*J: Is he about this height (Janet indicates a small boy about two feet high). He's wearing a sailor suit, we're going back.*

*R: I'm getting his energy. I'm not seeing anything. I'm just feeling him.*

*J: He was running through long grass.*

*R: He was a toddler, something happened.*

*J: He was white, nicely dressed with pantaloons.*

*R: His hair was neat, light brown and swept over.*
*J: I've got water, a big house in the background.*

*R: I see a pond.*

*J: He tripped and fell into the pond. He hit his head and swallowed water from the pond and drowned. People calling out for him. He was a curious little two-year-old. Mousey hair.*

*R: He's pointing at something. He's pointing because he was not verbal, he was deaf. Not saying anything. Deaf and mute. Go to the sunshine light. He's gone.*

*3. 2 March 2022 meeting.*

*A Ukranian soldier passes suddenly.*

*R: I've got a military person. He didn't know he'd crossed. When we were talking (before this meeting started) he knelt down in front of me and wanted to know what happened. I connected with him telepathically and told him he was shot, and I'm also seeing an explosion. He jumped out of his body. I was telling him he'd crossed over and died. He was upset because he'd just started. His intention was to protect his homeland. He didn't have the opportunity to serve Ukraine. He is a young man, about thirty. He gave me his name but I can't pronounce it.*

*J: Has he got dark hair?*

*R: Has he got a prominent nose? Medium built, average height, five foot ten or eleven. He's very sad. He's finding it difficult to come to terms with it.*

*J: He's showing me troops and tanks. They are all running on adrenalin.*

*J: He speaks.*

*E: 'It all happened very quick, we didn't have much chance to prepare, although the government should have allowed us to get prepared as everyone knew it would happen. All of a sudden it came out of nowhere, the military fire. I will never see my family again.'*

*R: He needs to go. Your family will be looked after.*

*J: He's gone.*

*4. 1 May 2023 meeting.*

*USA Southern States, 1860s. A young girl dies of fever.*

*J: Little white girl cared for by Black wet nurse. She's got a frilly dress on, a Shirley Temple lookalike. She's got a frilly dress, she's in the deep south, a couple of hundred years ago.*

*R: She looks like the girl from* Little House on the Prairie*.*

*J: She's also showing me a plantation with the Black slaves. There's her nanny, and she got so attached to her. When they reached a certain age, the children were told the nanny was her slave. Some children accepted that and some didn't.*

*R: Yeah, I saw her, she had nice clothes. She had a fever, a sudden death, she went quickly.*

*J: Are you getting a fire, or a thunderstorm?*

*R: I have her with a fever, I saw myself bathing her forehead in a fever. It was night outside, there was a storm, lightning. The blacks around her were caring for her. The room had gas light, darkened out in the corners. Thunder outside. There was blame about how she became ill; they blamed her Black carer. While a few of the slaves got the fever they lived and the girl died.*

*She was pretty, about nine or ten years old. All the helpers were in the room with her. The parents were outside the room. She's sitting over there with you, Rosie, in the room. It was a very long time ago. She passed very quickly with the fever. She actually used the word 'Mam'. That's how she would have called me. They would have looked after the little girl and made to leave their own children to look after the white girl. She would have had to breastfeed the white child when she was a baby. She'd have to let her own children go without, and other Black mothers would feed the carer's babies. They would be the wet nurse.*

*She's stroking my face. She's skipping, she was a lively little girl. She has a little boy with her. A little Black boy. She's pulling him and saying, 'Come with me.' He looks very skinny, not well nourished. She would have played with these kids. Some of them Black children were her half-siblings. He's saying he was beaten by the lady of the house. He was about five years old and used to carry water. If he spilt the water, he would get a good beating.*

*R: Go with your friend. You will feel a lovely energy. She is not like those people. Go with the girl. He's coming over, the girl's leading him. She said, 'One, two, three, jump.' They've gone.*

*5. 18 March 2021 meeting.*

*Dolphins tried to save a surfer.*

*J: I see a surfer being carried out to sea during bad weather. The dolphins tried to save him. They are very spiritual we're on the coast of Australia.*

*R: Got a very bad feeling, I think there is more to his story.*

*J: I think the board hit him on his head. People were there, they could have saved him.*

*R: What he's giving me is that someone told him not to go that day, feels like a loved one. A voice telling him not to go, the waves were behaving differently that day with a combination of wind and currents. He went against advice. He's saying he's at one with the dolphins. He was lucid. The dolphins were all around him when he died. He's talking about all these dolphins; he was quite big, athletic looking, good, strong physique.*

*J: I'm getting the Gold Coast. He wants to go. Let's cross him into the light. He's got his surfboard under his arm.*

*R: This young man is good looking with a bit of a swagger about him, and he knew it. His wetsuit stopped at the knees. Go to the light, he's swaggering and showing off. He kept talking about the dolphins.*

*6. 30 August 2023 meeting.*

*A teenage boy drowns by a weir.*

*R: At first it looks funny. Why would a person be standing on top of a dam? He fell in it. It wasn't deliberate, it was the way he fell. It wasn't a jump, a slip. Not pushed. Not suicide.*

*J: It looks like a weir. (Where water/rivers come together in a controlled way but it is very tempestuous.) That's what I've got. It's like trees hanging over.*

*R: I'm not seeing trees, I'm seeing a person falling down into the water. It could have been an accident, like a prank that went wrong. I say it's a 'he' I'm looking from a distance where you see someone doing a somersault. It wasn't a deliberate push more like a scare on a friend who lost his balance. He's standing on something, not like a bridge, a jetty or shelf into the water.*

*J: You could be walking along a ledge near the river near the weir where the flow of the water is very fast. Boys were running along the ledge and something went wrong. They could be playing on it. It would be slippery. They tried to grab him but he went over. It's teenage boys.*

*R: He's coming in. Good-looking boy, dark hair. He's stepped out of the water and he's soaking wet, dripping. Dark-brown hair.*

*J: The others tried to get him out, but the rush of the water took him away. The water looks harmless but it's powerful.*

*R: He's standing there. Go over to the lady.*

*J: He's got green water weeds all over him and down his throat. He's got big eyes. Good-looking boy. He's just looking around. No idea where and when. Not London, somewhere in the countryside, a small village.*

*R: This is not now, a while back. His trousers, brown corduroy. A voice is saying, 'C'mon, Mrs, get on with it.'*

*R: Walk towards the lady, step into the light. Get close enough to feel that warm energy, and as you feel that warm energy, the light will get stronger. Don't be fearful. The light is pulling you gently, lovingly. There's a kindness to it as well. It's your time to go. I know his mother's passed because he's saying, 'My mam.'*

*J: I've got a female saying, 'Come, child, come.'*

*R: It's time to rest, your mother and sister are waiting for you.*

*J: He's gone.*

*7. 3 March 2021 meeting.*

*A Leeds United football supporter dies in a car crash.*

*R: I saw someone a little while ago. He jumped in and punched the air, it was as if he was heading a ball. He's singing, 'We Are the Champions'. There's a football club that sings that. He's in a football kit, he's showing me a team – Leeds United.*

*Long-sleeved shirt, on someone's shoulder, as if they have won something.*

*J: I'm getting he was killed in a car accident. That's what they're giving me.*

*R: Good-looking young man. Hair swept to one side. He was a footballer. I'm seeing him in black and white – in the time of the 1970s. Rounded collar, loose shirts.*

*J: What colour is his kit? Could have been a supporter. R: The kit would have shown the era. He's going to meet his mum; his mum has crossed over. She hadn't passed at the same time but later.*

*J: The car was going fast and it skidded and smashed on the motorway. I don't know if he was alone in the car. He's smiling as he passed. He put the thumbs up. He was coming from a football match and kept saying, 'We won, we won'. That's why he's singing 'We Are the Champions'.*

*R: He was a cheeky lad. Turned round towards me, stuck his tongue out, go on, meet your mum.*

*J: He's bent down to do his shoelaces. There was someone with him. He's gone. It's like he was looking for them. He's gone.*

*8. 1 May 2023 meeting.*

*Performer falls from a high wire.*

*J: I've got someone here.*

*R: Do you want to say who you've got? Janet's laughing. Rosie, I've got someone here with bandy legs, like a rubber man. I'm getting the sense he would play tricks on someone like a contortionist. I want to feel an overwhelming sense of sadness. He's not telling me why.*

*J: He's here, he's just into my aura. He's very sad. In another country. Got a sun-kissed skin. It's like he's been in purgatory for some time. He's talking about the high wire. He walked the high wire. He's going over a bridge, very high over water. He had an accident. It happened very quickly. Lived in South America. He's sighing. He's been with Rosie for some time. He smiles, it's like he's on his journey now. Getting emotional. He seems to think that you (Rosie) have got to do it. To send him over. Because she's the beacon. I'm the light. They've never said this before – you are the beacon – I am the light.*

*J: All of a sudden, he's getting it now, how it works. He's got the hump with us because he was told to go to the light and you haven't done anything. He's smiling away. He's ready. He's clapping now. He's going home.*

*R: Move on now. Take the first step, feel the energy of the light, a warm fuzzy feeling. Go to meet your family. I'm going to say the Lord's Prayer. He still wants to talk. He hasn't gone.*

*He speaks to Steve: There is good fortune coming to you. Your light is bright I would like to travel within your light. To Rosie: I thank you, young lady, for allowing me to travel with you for so long. I will now depart.*

*R: Find your peace.*

*J: He won't go.*

*R: He has something else to say. He has not been in a physical body for some time now.*

*E: It's the warmth and the love here. It was very healing, you forgot about your worries and concerns. I will go there is a light. They are urging me to come forward. I take my leave.*

*R: Go to the light. The energy of the performer speaks:*

*E: 'I want to say before I leave: May the God, the peace and the love consume each and every one of you so you will be protected in the work you do. You are the light workers, the soldiers, the Spirit, so you can deliver your energies back to the core. I will now depart.'*

*J: He's gone.*

This might sound odd. Even though Soul Rescue is rooted in trauma and sadness, the meetings are often uplifting. This is because the energies are moments away from rejoining their greater selves. They have been waiting to reconnect and to be whole again. This is the joy and happiness. The energies like to tell their stories before they depart with smiles on their faces.

These words capture the dynamics of Rosie and Janet working together. Rosie is the beacon attracting the souls. Janet is the light that is the onward gateway to the realms.

'Because she's the beacon. I'm the light. They've never said this before – you are the beacon – I am the light.'

## Blog

*Shine Your Light*

Your spirituality shines. Shines like a homing beacon. It's your divine light that Spirit sees. Spirit doesn't see your physical, material form. They are sensitive to the love light you emit. Happiness and positivity shine brightly. This is especially so when you direct your mental energy towards them and their world. We are spirits on an earthly stage. By thinking of them we bridge the gap. Our Spirit is calling home.

We've asked our guides to describe what they see when viewing us. The answer is in the sky above, in the vista of stars, planets and glorious celestial activity. Look at the night sky above. See the millions of tiny dots of light above the wisps of clouds. To Spirit, we are those dots of light. We are those human spirits who are sending out spiritual signals of light. Their brightness is an indication of how we are feeling, elated or depressed; the beam can flow from dull to searingly bright.

In our minds we know that light conquers dark. That being downcast darkens our mood. That turning on the light of hope we can crawl away from despair. Smiling, helping, hugging, directs light to those in need, they inject light into dark. Your light is your human Spirit working in unison with the universe. Your kindness and consideration are a powerful restorative tonic to every element of the world around us.

The next time you're feeling low and night is drawing close

around you, look into the sky. Instead of tracts of darkness, see the million upon million points of light and take comfort.

Spirit is with you.

## Coming Next

*Universal Friends*

We are part of the universe. Surely, we can't be the only living beings in this infinite space? There is a mental communication beyond the clouds. This next chapter contains messages from our universal friends. They may surprise you.

# Eleven

## Universal Friends

*Guiding Light, a Distant Traveller*

Here are four messages from the universe. As the energies travel vast distances, they need to adjust their lighter energies to blend with our denser ones. This is why they use the one name of Guiding Light, who will speak on behalf of a group of energies, to represent them. The messages are in date order and have not been edited. You will read the text exactly as received.

*17 October 2022*

Communication received during a training meeting with Michael.

*Guiding Light*

> *Good day, my friends. I have come from a different dimension. I am a spiritual energy who comes from afar. I wanted to come and greet the new visitor (Michael). You have many energies around you. It will take time for you to unlock those energies and for them to come through to you and start talking through your vocal cords. You may be alarmed that you may hear voices talking through you from another planet, so I wanted to forewarn you. Do not be afeared or afraid because nothing in going to happen to you. We are long gone. We are that speck of energy that is from another realm, we have to do a lot of tweaking to adjust the energies. At times we want to see what's happening in your world. These energies are in the ether, and they travel many light years away. We have to work on the consciousness of the person we are linking with so we can use their vocal cords and learn their dictionary (vocabulary). So, my friend, it takes quite a long time. When I first made my entrance just now there was a lot of funny noises. I find it pleasurable now. Never be afeard when our lives have ended; we go back into the ether, you are not going to utter any words that may cause offence. You will learn a lot.*

*You are ready. Your light is there and your images in your mind are there. When I say the word images, they are photographs, they are stills, they've got a lock on them. When you start to develop, the stills will have movement because energy does have movement, they have fluidity. They will come back into your aura. You have an extremely good future in front of you and you will live and breathe with the Spirit with the energies around you for a very long time. Everything will start to make sense and you will wonder how many energies will live within your auric field. You will be able to give words to many people and make sense to many people. It is not you. It is the many energies that are going to choose you. They haven't been strolling around in the spiritual universe. They have chosen you for a very long time. My words need to cease now.*

*What I want to say about the universe is immense it goes on forever. Your globe is tiny. The universe goes on forever; there are many thousands of energies out there, and many planets are evolving. There are others that have exceeded their lifetimes. We are out there. We are not on scooters or on spaceships. I wouldn't have spoken this language. I just want to point a finger in front of me and say that you have a very exciting future in front of you spiritually. You will be in awe of all the work you will be able to process through your own mind and vocal cords.*

*9 January 2023*

## *Life on Other Planets*

Welcome, my friend, we come with much love, peace and

*energy. So that we can connect with your energies to relay down much information from our world and indeed so we can have conversations with each and every one of you.*

*As your earth spins on its axis around the universe along with many other planets that are out there, you reach out but cannot touch because they are too far. People look up to the sky to see if there is anything that would give them an inkling of if there is other life on other planets. My friend, this is an impossibility for the naked eye to see. People send up their rockets, their missiles. Even they would not be able to touch them. Have you ever wondered why another planet would not want to be seen or touched? They are not ready yet for invasion from the earth or from any other planet. They are eternal. Just like your lives, they are eternal; they go round and round and when there is a break, it is the end of a life on earth. That life returns to Spirit. The stars are all in alignment, going around your earth, not wanting to touch.*

*People are very inquisitive, especially on the earth. It is part of man's nature, being full of thoughts and wanting to ask questions. This is good. If you do not ask the questions, you do not get the answers. The questions are there to be asked. Man is always interested in what he cannot reach, cannot touch. If something is out of his grasp, he immediately wants to make contact, to touch it. And to be able to control. It is part of wanting to be in control. Man will never be satisfied and man always wants to know and that is a good thing.*

*From where I come from or from where I reside is a*

*very dark part of the universe that man would never be able to touch or see. We have our minds, our thoughts and our communication, my friend. That's how we find ourselves within the spiritual realms, within the ether, the atmosphere, the universe. As has been said to you many times before you are in the ether that surrounds your earthly planet that can reach out further and further. Imagine you go into space with no gravity. You would float and float. Imagine there is a band that keeps you within the influence of the earth.*

*I want you to listen to the words I'm going to say. Many people talk about aliens. They may say to someone who has Mediumistic skills, 'Have you ever been contacted by aliens?' Alien is a word that has been conjured up on the earth. It means something that is quite different and not usual, not used to. This is where man's inquisitiveness comes in. They look up to the skies and see the stars and planets. Are there other life forms?*

*Of course, there are life forms but not as you would imagine it. It's not as if you'd see eye to eye and say welcome. It has been said when energies have come through that man is backward. We feel that is an insulting thing to say to another universe, to people who have only been surviving for thousands and thousands of years, as there is much to learn when you're starting from scratch. And there is an awful amount for people to learn. For a universal energy to come through and say that man is backward and has much to learn, I feel that is quite insulting. From the place where we resided. We, too, had much to learn.*

*23 January 2023*

*The Voice of the Collective*

*Guiding Light*

*Once again, we come with love and friendship. We work with you. You work with us. We work jointly. We cannot do this without you. You cannot do this without us. We as a Collective look forward to coming through and blending our energies with you on the earth. We as the Collective work with many Mediums upon the earth worldwide.*

*We don't stick to one part of your globe. We blend our energies in with anyone we feel will be compatible with ours. We work with everyone differently, according to the way their energies are structured and according to the way we will be able to get the best from them at a particular moment in time. We work in conjunction with the guides of this channel (Janet). It is a joint affair. People like to see the Collective as aliens. People upon your earth like to depict aliens as creatures that look completely different and are formed completely different from how you are. We are beings from another universe. People expect us to come through and speak with a different tongue, a different language.*

*We have to take the time and effort to tune in with the energies we wish to work with. This takes a long time. We would have visited this energy a long time ago to be able to blend in with her energy and tune in with her brain waves so we can use her vocabulary. It would not have been possible for us to use our language as it would be unknown to her, be 'alien' to her. This way it would be easier for us all to understand each other.*

*There is a reason why we come and converse. It is because all the planets are in misalignment and at times this can cause disruption. The planets will start to come into alignment and there will be a shift in patterns towards the earth. Things will start to settle down. Some people do not take much notice on what is happening in the universe. They should. There is a shifting in the way the planets are aligning and this will make people feel better. It is of great importance in how the planets are behaving. You are greatly affected by all the energy that has built up. If you understand what is happening outside your planet, you will understand what is happening to the universe as a whole.*

*Energies we are. We are from the Collective. We often come as the Collective; as we blend all our energies together, they become stronger and we will blend our energies in with more people on the earth. We shine the light on everyone. The atmospheric pressure on the earth is also very important, and the pressure in yourself on the way you are living and working. We try to home in on the people we are going to converse with to go deep within your thoughts to pick out those subjects that will be important to you.*

*28 January 2023*

*We Are Not Aliens, Only Unknowns*

*In a previous meeting when Michael was there, an energy came through from the Collective, speaking about the universal friends and the universe. We picked up on Michael's mind that evening because that had been on Michael's mind.*

*Sometimes we do this for clarification or other people as there may be somewhere there who is listening in the meeting who may have a thought on something within the spiritual realms. We will touch on that so it may help someone who is thinking about that topic. We are there for everyone about the universal energies. Spiritual energies and universal energies are one thing that people find it hard to understand; they find it hard to separate the two.*

*You see, you've got your earth, you've got your planet. Imagine going out for a thousand miles outside your earth. Imagine this is an invisible outer layer, but instead of an atmospheric sphere, it represents the spiritual realms surrounding your world. If you go further and further out into the universe, the idea of a surrounding belt holds true. Every planet that may have had a lifeform on it would have a notional one-thousand-mile belt around it. You've had visits from your universal friends saying they've had to travel many light-years to reach you. They've had to let their energies adjust to our atmosphere because of the massive distances they've covered to reach our spiritual realm. Does this make sense?*

*This is where some people see spirituality as a religion. As this has been classed as a law by your government. Many see religion as the link with Jesus and God. They associate God as the father of Jesus. They see religion only relating to this small ball of energy that is your planet. They can't see or think of anything outside the earth. So, when people start talking about aliens they shut down as they feel this is being disrespectful to Jesus and God and disrespectful to the Holy*

*Spirit. This is why we refer to them as universal friends and not aliens. They will be friends who are visiting that spiritual belt within your atmosphere.*

*You don't have to go to churches to know you have that particle of God within you. That we refer to as the Creator, the divine light, the giver of life. It is that little light, that spark, that is your Spirit. They start to associate Spirit with Jesus and Mary, these are the Christians that see God as the father of his Holy Son. They cannot step outside of that teaching for fear of being disrespectful to their faith.*

*You have the other religions on the earth. We know there are many denominations that believe in us. They feel that the God they are worshipping was the head of their church on the earth. They know that when you go back to Spirit it is all the same. Some people are open-minded to the fact that there may be aliens. Since the world began, people have always looked up into the moon, the sky, the planets, and would wonder if there are other people living there.*

*It is the inquisitiveness, especially with people who are doing this kind of work. Sometimes the word 'alien' puts fear into people. Fear of the unknown. They do not know what to expect, so they judge an alien as someone or something that is not good and the soul within that energy is not good. It can be quite the opposite, if truth be known. Just because they are called aliens, it does not mean they intend you harm. It is a figure of speech that goes into people's minds. You only have to use a word out of context and it can cause offence. The same can be said with the word religion. Some people shut off when that word is said.*

*We hope that being spiritual overcomes any negativity.*

## Blog

*Love Lasts Longer than a Lifetime*

Love is in your heart and in your head. Access the memories inside your mind. Think of a loved one. Instantly they are there. Mother, father, son, daughter, lovers, best friends, grandparents, anyone and everyone whom you've loved are living and breathing once more. The pictures run. The images cascade. The memories flow.

These loves, these emotions are of this lifetime. This life is an eternal storehouse of emotions. They are ingrained in your mind and Spirit. They last forever. Your Spirit is indestructible. The thought energy that immediately recaptured that tender touch, that loving embrace, that soft scent, that gentle voice, that look of love that you knew was only for you will endure forever.

Your soul is your emotions. Your Spirit is your eternal being. Put the two together and you are a complete human Spirit, a spiritual being.

Now turn those thoughts in another direction.

Like you, your loved ones are eternal. As a spiritual being you were born with psychic ability. It's like being born with your own psychic toolbox. Some elements in the toolbox are so obvious you don't realise they are spiritual gifts. Consciousness and your conscience are two. Your imagination and intuition are two more. Many of us are not aware of or try to develop our sixth sense. A Spiritual Medium has been trained to explore these gifts of intuition.

Through teaching, regular practice, and often years of experience, a Spiritual Medium can direct the power of thought energy to achieve a connection and open a channel of communication with Spirit. This is where the flow of evidence comes from. This is how you can get proof that consciousness continues after physical death. This is where you are given personal details that describe a friend or loved one, a relative or person you have known.

This is when you know in your heart that love lasts longer than a lifetime.

## Coming Next

*Meet the Guides*

Our greatest thanks to the Spirit Guides within the group of eight, members of Running Water's circle and highly evolved guides who have visited us and contributed to the writing of this book. Some were the same guides of our first two books, some are new. They're waiting on the next page to say hello.

# Twelve

## Meet the Guides

The descriptions that follow show the character and 'humanity' of these guides to show they are not imaginary fantasy creatures but were once flesh and blood. As you read these pieces, remember that in Spirit, 'thought' can assume material and physical properties as if they are happening in the real world. The guides have taken this opportunity to tell their stories in Spirit and on earth.

Apart from guides who at one time lived on earth, we have had the incredible benefit of being contacted by angels, archangels, and celestial energies. This involvement speaks to the infinite nature of the spiritual world. As our contact with Spirit is constant, different guides join us to provide help and guidance when needed or when we have new Mediums who are accompanied by their personal guides.

The Group of Eight Native American Indians. In their own words, this is how the Group would like to introduce themselves:

*To the reader: Our group has been formed in our world for many decades. We are made up of eight guides, all of whom have been working together for the sole reason to help guide and teach those people on your earth that choose to work alongside us in the capacity of Spiritual Mediums. For the newly developing Mediums there are guides who are taught by us to lead them on their new journey. These would be trained guides who reside on a lower level; they are still being trained by us while they are training and working with the developing Medium.*

*On this journey we have communicated through thought. Our words are transmitted to the mind of this Medium, who in turn will deliver it to the writer. These Mediums were chosen by us for this work for their combined energies and strength. It is a journey that will lead them further on their spiritual pathway.*

*We all have our different roles to play; we all have different personalities. Each one of us is here for a reason. There is the one with patience, one who is impulsive, one who likes to be the balance, one who likes to have hearty discussions, one who will push hard, one who has an open mind, and one who will disagree. Then there is the leader, the overseer of all, the wise one whom we all look up to, yet we are all equal. This group is a fine balance of energies that have chosen to work together in order for us to pass on our knowledge.*

*We work with many Mediums on your earth, and we work differently with every Medium we choose according to their abilities. These two Mediums we have chosen for a project to explain about our world in simple terms, a project where it would get the interest of many who otherwise would dismiss us. It is a platform for people to work upon. If you wish to explore more of our world there would be more knowledge and literature available, which would be able to widen your mind and interest; we wish you all well on your journey.*

Introducing individual members of the Eight:

*The Group have gathered once again, and we feel it is about time we made our introductions. It's been spoken to you that the head of our group is someone famous in your world. We would like to take this opportunity to explain about this great leader. He resides and takes the head of many groups in our world. He is not the highest Spirit in our existence; he still has many levels to conquer. His Native American Indian name is Tatanka-Iyotake, of the Hunkpapa Lakota. He is also known as Sitting Bull. My friend, you would be aware that highest status goes to the divine light, the infinite being. We do not have labels in our world as to who is better than anyone else. It's merely explaining the order of longevity back in our world.*

*He is a very wise master and has gathered much valuable knowledge which in turn he teaches to his pupils. These are other spirits evolving towards the eternal light and along the way wish to gain as much knowledge as possible in order to filter this back to your earth. It is the knowledge from our world that helps people in your world progress and for them to make changes for the future.*

*Imagine on your earth a professor of infinite knowledge. He takes great pleasure in sharing that knowledge with anyone who is eager to listen and learn. He will teach groups of great advancement, also groups going back down the scale to beginners. There is no one who he will not help.*

*He has many helpers who work alongside him who also in turn head certain groups of their own. Each group undertake many different subjects, some of which differ greatly from one group to the next, but whatever the subject, it is equally important as another.*

*To the right side of our leader sits Blue Flame, Five Arrows, Black Feathers, Red Arrow, Rain Cloud, Brown Bear and Morning Mist, who will be on the left-hand side, thus securing the circle. Running Water, White Cloud, Wang Chang and White Bear are guests of this group and are invited to sit in amongst us. Behind us will be our helpers, which Singing Winds would be one of them, and not forgetting Wang*

*Chang's helpers, also there are others too numerous to mention but equally important.*

*This message is from Singing Winds, who wishes to pass on this knowledge from the leader of the group. The teepee has been assembled with the members of the group. The head of the group wishes to extend his blessings to you and to tell you more of his life on earth:*

*My dear friend, when I was on the earth living my life, I encountered many misfortunes. We were living a peaceful existence for a short time until the white man came and decided that everything they saw and touched belonged to them. They were blinded by anything that was new to them. They saw our people and our way of life an intrusion into their way of life. It was never in their intelligence to join us and be interested in our ways and learn from us. All they wanted was to take from us and for us to fall into their way of living.*

*We were of the land they stole from us, claiming they had the right to take away everything that we worshipped and valued. They said it was the 'new land' and they had a right to make claims upon it. It was our heritage, our forefathers worked hard to instil pride into each and every one of us. The white man called us savages because we were talking in our mother tongue. They forget, my friend, it was they who were the invaders. They ridiculed our rituals, which we had been performing for hundreds of years, claiming we were backward and was forced to learn the white man way.*

*We retaliated and fought against the injustice that was being put upon us. I stood tall and held my ground for the love of my people and the land that we grew to love. I was always true to my word. We were proud people. I fought and won battles and even joined their side to prove that we could all live and work beside each other in good faith. My reward came in the form of betrayal from the people I came to trust.*

*That was in my time. Since that time many moons ago, people say they have learnt from past mistakes and want to learn about our ways and rituals. Many of us have become famous names upon your earth. We are now looked up to instead of being looked down upon. We are worshipped and treasured. The lands we fought so hard to keep for our homes belong to no one. They belong to the earth. Our spirits and memories are embedded upon the soil that took so many lives protecting it.*

*My friend, I came to Spirit harbouring no ill will. I forgave those who betrayed me and my people. From then on, every Spirit that has joined me in my world has had to learn how to forgive themselves for the atrocities they would have committed on your earth. They have had to sift through every emotion they possess and learn from all the mistakes they made. Even I would have had to go through the same process. To forgive those who have done ill towards you means you can walk forward instead of always looking back. Your Spirit will grow in strength. You will gain knowledge and wisdom. You will be able to embrace any new knowledge that is to be put before you. You will shine.*

*My role is to teach in a way where vast knowledge is*

*channelled into the minds of those who are ready to receive. Judgement is not for me or any Spirit to place upon anyone. The day of judgement comes, my friend, when the physical existence finishes and the spiritual one begins. That is when mankind have to own up to the mistakes they committed when on the earth. The journey to the infinite light can prove to be an enlightening one where the Spirit will truly gain a wealth of wisdom.*

Singing Winds wanted to add his own account of the teepee, the group's meeting place. He describes his entrance after being away from the group for a while. Spirit Guides remember themselves as we remember them when they were on earth. This is true for our loved ones who have passed recently, as well as those like Singing Winds who passed hundreds of years ago. During the writing of this book, the group of eight held 'virtual' meetings in their teepee or in the formal setting of an auditorium. Spirit uses these mental links to help us visualise the proceedings in terms we can understand. As you know, there are no solid structures in a world of mind and thought. It is the energy of imagination. Singing Winds is Steve's brother in Spirit. It may help us to think we're watching a cinema screen as guides describe gatherings in their world.

*The Teepee: It is quite large. The opening is to the right of you; in the middle it looks like logs but not a big blazing fire; on the floor, all around the sides, are skins all scattered around and in the middle looks like loose stones where the fire is placed in the centre.*

*Sitting to my left is Running Bear. He has a fur hat on his head (it hasn't got a tail) and a short fur coat; he is looking at me and smiling and says, 'Where have you been? We have been waiting for you for a long time.' I'm a tall Indian warrior, quite slim, rugged skin and of good years. I have scars on my face through battle. I sit down facing Running Bear and make a tribal sign. I would have been killed in battle, and my name is Singing Winds. I was from the Cherokee tribe and of the character that nothing would stop me in my tracks. If a thought came into my head, it would drive me along until my job was done. I was fearless but compassionate, impulsive and quick to judge, a trait that has had to be refined now I am no longer on the earth.*

*There is to be a meeting. I stay sitting, and one at a time, others are filing into the teepee and we do a strange handshake. I can't understand the language at all but there is a lot of laughter around; the flap opens and in comes the leader. I know this because there is a lot of respect. He exudes charisma and importance. Running Bear is talking to me in tongues and we laugh then all goes serious. The leader has a long pipe (it's thin, more like a reed rather than a clay pipe we would envision). It is now being passed round. There is complete silence and peace. The meeting begins.*

*They are talking about past battles for land, they are speaking very quickly. They are pleased that I have joined them now after such a long time. The meeting is now over; they all seemed pleased with the way it went. I rise and walk through the flap; outside waiting for me are others on horseback. They are younger than I am, my horse is ready, and I mount. After farewells, we ride away.*

This is how Janet described how the gathering assembles in the auditorium that looks like a semi-circular ancient theatre with aisles, banks and rows of seats:

'Imagine an auditorium above your head; it's like they put me in the ring and I watch all the guides file in. The higher guides take the front seats and the rest all sit behind. The head of the guides always sit on the front row in the middle and they fan out accordingly. White Cloud sits next to him as he is Steve's guide. Wang Chang will sit on the other side, and I have Running Water with me in the circle. Running Water has to be with me because he is my guardian and protector. When a question is put to the group, it's known that they argue amongst themselves and they can become very vocal. Other spirits arrive to listen and learn from the proceedings.'

### *White Cloud*

This is White Cloud's first message channelled by Janet to Stephen:

*My friend, I have been with you many years. I have witnessed sadness and distress within your life and the search for peace. It can be hard at times for us as a guide when we have to watch our chosen Medium make mistakes, it has to be done, it is life, it is how people learn. We choose our time when we guide you onto a clearer pathway, it has to be done with your choosing, when you realise that the time is right for you to make amends. Your search has taken you along pathways of inquisitiveness and understanding.*

*I have been there all the time, leading you from one path to another until we knew the time was right to bring you to your rightful pathway. Many times, I remained a silent guide, the time is now right for me to introduce myself to you. My role within the group is one of a guest, my status in my world would be one of the same as the group. As Running Water is the main guide of Janet, I am the main guide for you, Stephen. There are many others, which include Singing Winds; as time goes on, we will introduce others who are an important part in your spiritual life.*

*When choosing who we are to follow, we choose people of similar character; we have many of the same traits; we choose like for like; this is so our energies can blend to the fine-tuning we need for complete harmonisation. My time on earth would have been long in years, my status within my tribe would have been an important one where there were many decisions which would have been placed before me. We would have travelled at times for survival. That would have meant my one aim was to look after and care for others within our fold, thus enabling me to hide my sensitive nature and adopt one of assertiveness, and at times, arrogance.*

*I wished and eventually found peace and contentment. We work together differently than that of Running Water and Janet, it is necessary for the blending of a continuous partnership. The Group are and always will play an important part in our journey. I will consult them many times where there will be new turnings in our direction. We are good leaders. We are there in complete friendship and will never lead you on a wrong pathway. White Cloud, Cherokee Indian.*

### *Running Water*

*I am known to Janet as Running Water; I am her main guide. We have been in partnership since she was brought back to this earth. My energies remained silent until the time was right for her to join us on our journey. A journey which has had its ups and downs, happy times and sad times, we are a partnership. Our energies have bonded and blended in a way where trust has been firmly placed between us. We lead, she follows. That is true friendship, believing and trusting. Her journey has only just begun; everything that went before was just a rehearsal until the joining of energies were entwined in order for the main work for Spirit to begin. The work now has begun.*

*I am a Native American Indian who came from the Navaho tribe. We were peaceful people who only hunted for survival. We faced many trials throughout our lives. There was nothing we could not overcome. I had two wives, both of whom I outlived, four sons and three daughters and many grandchildren. My time in Spirit has been spent training and learning. Janet is my first Medium for whom I am the sole protector, her main guide, as I like to say, the one who pulls the strings. We are a joint partnership, we do not control, we work together.*

*It is my responsibility to protect her. She works with us for the purpose of channelling. We have spoken many words to many people and have produced much evidence. During this time, it was never my intention to give clairvoyant messages. We in Spirit only wanted to talk about our world and answer any questions. It was quickly established that certain people on your earth were more interested in their material life; in order for me to develop with Janet, that was the path that we had to follow. So, my friend, for many years we have had many meetings in this way; eventually we put her onto a pathway where she could develop her gift in a way where I was not needed.*

### *Wang Chang*

*He is on a higher level. Wang Chang is a guest of the circle. He is a venerable teacher. We are aware you have been acquainted with him, once met, never forgotten. He is from the Ming Dynasty and is a very clever and wise guide. You will have many conversations with him over the years. Wang Chang is his own master. He is an important visitor to my group; he will come and go as he wishes and when he feels he is needed.*

### *Canuji*

*He is the most serious of the guides within the circle. He is very caring and a great healer, often the description of a Witch Doctor or Medicine Man is used to describe him. He has a team of workers who are healers and like to use old-fashioned methods of healing; grasses and herbs are his main instruments. His symbol is of a Black Panther. If you are in pain or ailing in health, then you are at liberty to visualise this symbol; he has given you permission. He would have been placed on your earth in the region of East Africa. His journey back to Spirit was in his second decade due to an infection from a wound in his arm. He rarely speaks now within the group but he is always in attendance.*

*He is very sensitive in nature and is only interested in the health of any person in the meeting or their animals. He is very sincere in the role he plays and will be a rarity if he ever imparted with a message. Occasionally he will impart information about the health of someone who isn't present in the meeting. His main interest is to keep people well in mind and body. He is regarded as a prince amongst his people. His costume of the skin of the Black Panther maintains his position amongst his tribe. He is very proud; they were proud people.*

### *Abdullah*

*He would like to introduce himself personally and has been given permission:*

*Welcome, my friend. It is with great pleasure that my introductions can be directed from me personally. It's never been in my favour to have someone else speak for me. I have always liked to be known as the wise one, the fixer, the one who can sort out problems for another.*

*When it was my life on the earth, my geographical position was in North Africa, the country would be known to you as Egypt. My town has now been long gone, covered in dust and entwined within a city. My trade was that of a merchant in cloth and of many other items that would have been useful for the home. My other main purpose was that of money lender. People would come to me with all manner of problems, be it if their donkey's legs had buckled, or if the wife had committed adultery, or if they had no means to buy food for their children.*

*There was nothing I could not fix. People would travel for miles and days for my services to help them with their problems. Each night when it was quiet, I would walk into the desert and gaze towards the sky and consult the stars, the celestial beings. That was where my guidance would come from. The stars became my guardians, the whisperers, the helpers of all. I would relay any concerns to the stars and would be rewarded with the correct solution.*

*It was only when my Spirit came back to this world that I realised that all along it was the help from Spirit. They served me very well, my friend, so it was understood from the beginning that was my pathway to help your troubled earth. My part within the circle is enjoyable; I like to utter words, and I like to give my opinion. We will meet, my friend, when the dust has settled and the time is right.*

*The specialist role Abdullah likes to play within the circle is that of an advisor. The main purpose of his intervention is to give everyone hope that although at the time of hardship there is nothing that cannot be resolved. Every argument or altercation has two sides, and it is up to the parties involved to listen to each other with an open mind. He has a huge sense of humour. The reason he talks of vast distances between his clients and himself is to place in everyone's mind that at times of distress and anger there should be a cooling down period. This gives the mind time to absorb all that has gone on and to be able to come to a mutual decision. It is a subtle approach in advising people to think rationally rather than irrationally.*

### *Charlie*

*Charlie known as Charles Short, nicknamed Lofty, is from London's East End. He lived into his twenties and was taken from this earth in World War II in a bombing raid during the Blitz. He likes to tell his own story which will be given to you when you meet him. He is the most popular of the guides. His great sense of humour relaxes everyone, especially those who are feeling nervous. He's funny, cheerful and not too fond of authority. Charlie's very clever. His cheerful manner disguises how shrewd he is. He quickly reduces anxieties and gives meaningful messages.*

### *Josiah*

Josiah has a very sensitive energy and always gives assurance that all will be well in the world. He is a talented scribe. His eyesight is worsening after years of writing with his quill by candlelight. He loves nothing more than sitting on his veranda with his wife, Eliza, and having his daughter Ruth and son Ezra near him. They lived in Virginia in the 1860s.

This is his love poem to Eliza:

How my heart sings when I hear your voice
How my heart sings when I see your smile

You came into my life like an angel falling from Heaven
You are my own precious gift.
How I smile when I see you happy
How I am sad when I see you sad
You are mine to love and protect
You are my own precious gift
The colours of the rainbow
Dance around you like sparkling gems
Through the clouds the rays of the sun shine like a torch from
Heaven upon your hair
The wind brings colour to your cheeks like apples
You are my own precious gift
You light up my life
You lift up my soul
You fill my heart with love
You were sent to me and I to you
We are our own precious gifts to each other.

Josiah adds:

*Eliza would place all my poems and letters together, tie with string, and place in a cardboard box. When she was feeling melancholy, she'd take them out and read them over and over again.*

More recently, these guides have joined us.

*Two Jimmys and a Poet*

*We have two guides with the same name. Jimmy One has been with us for some time via the Running Water group link.*

*He was a soldier in the Ypres battles of the First World War trenches in 1917. He died from gangrene poisoning from an artillery wound. He was a Londoner. Jimmy is very astute and provides us with a great deal of wisdom and information. This is what Jimmy the soldier was saying about the war in Ukraine defending itself against the Russians:*

*'I've been around the war zone. When you're there, you get used to the horror but when you're apart looking in, it becomes commonplace. But when in with it, you adjust. The Spirit is an amazing thing you can adjust to the situation that's going on around you. When you're watching it on television you see the destruction and filth. When you're in it, you close your mind and get on with it. Over the centuries, there's always that one person who starts the wars. Power never wins. Destructive power never wins. It can't win, it's impossible. You can't allow the dictator of a country to become the ruler of the world. He didn't want that country and those people; he just wanted security for himself. To him, they were like flies he would swat away.'*

Michael introduced his guide Jimmy to the group, who is a very different character. He would talk about his past lives and the pain and anguish he suffered as a result of repeated torture. We won't linger on that because his strength and positivity was never crushed. You'll see by his energy and sense of humour:

*Ooh! Hello! You two again! You are so funny. I'm Jimmy, nice to see you again. I've been watching you all week, and I've been around you, young lady (Janet). You've been having fun with your daughter (Lucy). I've been listening to what you were saying, and I love the energy with your daughter. She seems a lot happier now, would you understand that? She has been very happy, very bubbly.*

*And you, sir. I feel there's been a happier sense with you. Your energy seems to be fun. Did you hear my voice being fun too? I just wanted to come and say hello. I didn't think I was going to come here today, but when I saw you two sitting there smiling, and I saw your light, so I really wanted to come. To say hello, and to tell you my name. I didn't tell you before, my name is Jimmy. I've been here for such a long time.*

The Poet, a fellow writer, said these first words to Steve:

*You are the energy I like to work with, the words I come through to you in the night and in the day and I would like to give you some more information as I would like to expand your vocabulary to the depth to describe our world in a way that only you can represent in the words, lingo and language that represents us the best. Words are energy from the universe from the creation, from the very beginning.*

*Words have energy, internal and external. Words come from a very long lineage. Your job is to make it simple for others. It's not dumbing down but to make it simpler to understand. We will come to you to help you describe our realms in a way to help them understand the complexity of our world. It is such a dynamic energy in the realms. There are realms within the realms. Remember, we are there in the night skies.*

We hope these excerpts will show you how in tune our guides are with our lives and their acute awareness of events happening in our world. They also attest to the care, love and learning they want to share with us.

## Blog

*Say Hello to Your Spirit Guide*

When you were little were probably told you had a guardian angel. That's true. You also have your own Spirit Guide. This is how Spirit Guides introduce themselves:

> *Spirit Guides have lived on earth. Guides may have experienced a number of earthly visits each one in a different human situation in different time periods and circumstances. As they have learnt so you will learn during your lifetime. You have one principal guide assigned to you. They will be with you from conception to passing. The role of the guide is one of love and friendship. They are there to help guide and protect. They will never judge.*

That message is from Black Feathers, a highly evolved Native American Indian guide. You have a primary guide who is your friend and supporter for all your life. At different phases in your life, you will probably have other guides helping you. These visiting guides would have experienced similar emotional situations as you are going through so they will give you their care and understanding to help you.

Black Feathers continues:

*It is a partnership of love and friendship. The blending of energies can work as one and be the best friend that would never let you down. This is natural in your world; the guides understand for they have also, at one point, been in an earthly existence. They have chosen this role. They are Spirit messengers whose only aim is to disperse the love and light from our world to yours.*

*Talk to your guides. Chat to them when you're feeling down. Thank them when you're exultant. Ask their opinion when making decisions. They are there for you. Over time and with the will, you can develop your spiritual self. Each earthly lifetime has been designed for you to experience human emotions as your Spirit evolves towards the divine light. With greater understanding, your light will shine brighter.*

## Coming Next

### *Closing Thoughts*

Four little letters. L o v e. They say it makes the world go round and the next world and the universe. Everything. We thank you from the bottom of our hearts for reading these past chapters as we come to the last, the shortest. Short enough to pass on this gift to you from Spirit. We hope all these words of love and learning will make a difference in the way you think of yourself, your friends and loved ones and has put a spring in your step.

# Thirteen

## Closing Thoughts

*One Life, Two Threads*

This book is for You. Spirit in human form. An immortal being.

We appreciate this duality of existence is difficult to accept. It will take time and personal evidence to gain acceptance. It's unlikely to happen until you have utter certainty. Not everyone is prepared to take that step and dare to believe in a twin identity. To know who you are and why you're living this life.

This time is part of a parallel progression of two intertwined lives, one mortal, one spiritual. Which over aeons of time, will lead to divine fulfilment in the Realms of Spirit. You will become as one in fellowship with your guides.

As a starting point, get the proof for yourself. Don't believe. Until you have evidence. Gain certainty. Have no doubt.

Listen to a Medium make the connection with loved ones you've lost. They are still with you, loving and caring for you. The Spiritual Medium would not know you or anything about you. It is up to them to give you that pearl of proof. For them to rock you back with the personal facts that only you know. Facts that could not be drawn by reading your mind or playing tricks. I explain what happened to me in my biography as I did not believe a word of all this until that fateful day.

For now, we want to share some more words direct from Spirit, to underline their connection with us. This is from Tomahawk; his words focus on spirituality being the ultimate belief.

*14 February 2020*

*Tomahawk*

*We want people to realise that we are linked with every*

*religious belief. We get dismissed by the leaders of the religions in their temples or synagogues or churches or wherever they are praying. We are dismissed; their parishioners are not allowed to believe in us. We do not mind in our world as every spiritual energy will believe when they come back and know the truth. We do not have to howl it from the rooftops; we like everyone to share through our writings.*

*We know that time is important in your world. But you've heard it from our world that you will have the time to move on and pass on the news and messages that we feel are important for people to learn and understand. All the poems and words in these books we will pass them on and share. Our work is for a vast group of people. We have an advantage over you on the earth as we are not disturbed by what people look like. We see people's lights. That's where we direct our thoughts and energies.*

Spirit see us in the same way as we see the millions of twinkling stars in the night sky. They do not see our mortal form. They don't see what we're wearing or what we're doing. It is our spiritual energy they sense as being aware of our soul's progress.

Live life full of love. Shine your light. Remember the words we began with. And will end with.

We are all visitors to this time, this place.
We are just passing through.
Our purpose here is to observe, to learn, to grow, to love
And then
We return home.

A closing prayer from Mary:

*From the Divine, from our world, from my heart, the heart of Mary, we give you an outpouring of love, peace and protection.*

*We give you wisdom, we give you courage, we give you strength in order to continue the battle of your lives because some like to see their lives as a battle.*

*It is a privilege to live a life on your earth. To be able to witness first-hand what it's like to live with one another.*

*How to share the love, to share the friendship and to share the peace.*

*From our world to yours, we send you much love.*
*Amen.*

# Appendix One

## Author Profiles

*Janet Neville*

When twenty-five years ago I walked through the doors of Barnes Healing Church, there was not even a hint in my mind of what was to follow. A few days before, a friend and I went to have a reading from a Medium – at that time, I would call them fortune tellers – this was because I had no idea or any interest in thoughts of the afterlife. In the reading, she told me that my pathway in life would become very spiritual and that I would walk along a very deep and meaningful journey with many guides. Once outside her house, laughter got the better of us because that was not what we were expecting to hear.

I wasn't bargaining on the force of the unseen forces that were to become my lifelong friends, so on that Sunday, out of curiosity, there we both were, sitting in the pews of this lovely church, wondering what on earth I was doing there. If I were to continue from everything that has happened to me since, the words would run into another volume.

The journey has become a most wonderful experience that has given me a lot of joy, pleasure and hope working alongside these invisible friends of mine. My main guide is Running Water; his tolerance and patience has paid dividends. He is of the energy who has guided me through years of teaching, learning, and understanding.

The first few years were taken up with channelling; this is where Running Water's energy uses my voice to allow verbal conversations to take place. These are messages from deceased spirits sent to loved ones left on earth. They are also messages of hope and enlightenment about the world of Spirit. During this time, other energies who channelled through me have become my lifelong friends.

When they felt it was time, I was directed to a circle in Kingston Spiritual Church to develop as a Spiritual Medium to work clairvoyantly and to develop as a platform Medium. After about four years I left the circle and eventually started to work on the platform in many of the churches and centres.

In 2016, my life was to change once again. My friend Bernadete asked if I would give a demonstration of Mediumship for her two circles; it was Christmas time, and she thought it would be nice to have a service just for them. She also invited along Steve, who at that time was a complete stranger to me. After the meeting, he approached me with an idea of the two of us joining forces to produce a book about how we are all spirits in a physical body and explain about the spiritual realms. So, another journey began. Since then, our lives have become a triangle of work, that is myself, Steve and Spirit; we have written our first book, *Being Spirit;* the second, *Believe in Spirit*, was published in 2021. *Immortal Spirit* will be published in 2025. Together we also have groups where we help others to develop and progress on their paths for Spirit. The whole experience is one of enjoyment, dedication and fulfilment.

*Steve Bridger*

In Janet, I've met someone with years of high-level experience as a Spiritual Medium. She is the communication channel between our two worlds. My role is to pass on those messages using the spoken and written word. The two of us work together and combine our separate skills to help people understand more about Spirit. And more about themselves.

Janet is the lynchpin receiving and writing all the content channelled from Spirit. I write the narrative flow and manage the content into chapter order. My Mediumship is the way our guides put ideas into my mind. Mainly during my sleep state.

In my adult life, I worked in advertising as an account executive. Sailed the Atlantic from Gibraltar to Antigua as part of a yacht delivery crew. Spent time working as a roadie for rock bands. Became a tour manager for acts in Europe, Dubai and Zimbabwe. Ran my own business in the UK gardening sector winning the New Product of the Year Award in 1999. Yes, there was a party. Wrote three books before I met Janet and we became co-authors.

I did not believe any of this. Until my negative, cynical approach was blown away one morning at the Kingston Upon Thames Spiritual Church. I realised I knew nothing about spiritualism. I was Mr Negative. As a child, I was sent to a Catholic school and force-fed doctrine to last several lifetimes.

I had a reading with a Medium. Fifteen minutes passed in silence. No messages, nothing. The Medium asked for a couple more minutes. Then everything changed. She accurately described my best friend. He was wearing our school uniform from the RAF Changi Grammar School in Singapore. His message was to ask our friends to stop being angry with him. He'd taken his own life. This is how I received my evidence, my proof. That was twenty-four years ago. Here I am, finishing this sentence after three books and 53,000 words with Immortal Spirit.

To you with love from Spirit and both of us.

Please Contact Us:
Email: spirit@beingspirits.com
Website: www.beingspirits.com
Facebook: www.facebook.com/beingspiritbook
Instagram: beingspirit1

# Appendix Two

## Spiritual Links – UK and International

Here are some links for more about spirituality.

*UK Spiritual Churches/Centres – Around London*

London Spiritual Mission: www.spiritualmission.co.uk
Kingston Spiritual Church: www.//kingstonsc.net
Barnes Healing Church: www.barneshealingchurch.co.uk
Maidenhead Spiritual Church:
www.maidenheadspiritualistchurch.com
Acton Spiritual Centre: Search on Facebook &
www.thespiritualist.org
Wimbledon Spiritual Church:
www.wimbledonspiritualistchurch.co.uk
UK Spiritual Organisations
UK Search Site: www.thespiritualist.org
Spiritual National Union: www.snu.org.uk
College of Psychic Studies: www.collegeofpsychicstudies.co.uk

The Spiritualist Association of Great Britain: www.sagb.org.uk
United Spiritualists: www.unitedspiritualists.org.uk

*International Links*

Canada: www.spiritualistchurchofcanada.com
USA: National Spiritual Association of Churches:
https://nsac.org
Australia: www.spiritualist-church.org.au
New Zealand: www.spiritualism.org.nz
India: Go Spiritual India: www. gospiritualindia.org
Reiki Healing Training
Reiki Academy London: www.reikiacademy.com
www.centreofexcellence.com
Helping the Planet
Fauna & Flora: www.fauna-flora.org
World Wildlife Fund: wwf.org.uk
WaterAid UK: www.wateraid.org